# MY
# MOTHER THE
# ARSONIST

Waldman House Press

# MY MOTHER THE ARSONIST

—— *&* ——

## *other toasty tales*

## *By Dave Wood*

Waldman House Press
Minneapolis

You may order single copies from the publisher. Try your bookstore first. Cover price plus $1.00 postage and handling.
Waldman House Press
525 North Third Street
Minneapolis, Minnesota 55401

Printed in the United States of America
First Printing, May 1988

ISBN: 0-931674-11-5

Drawings and design by Todd Grande

*For Ed Goodpaster*
*who got me into this mess*

# Acknowledgements

A book doesn't spring full-blown from the head of its author. For an attractive, readable, coherent book to see the light of day, many people must put their talents and energies to the task.

Production of this book has been blessed with a crew of enthusiastic and skillful people who massaged, teased, tickled and made the best of the material the author shoved their way.

I would like to offer special thanks to that crew: To my colleague Diane Osby, who speedily prepared a meticulous manuscript. To Ingrid Sundstrom, who edited the copy with enthusiasm and skill. To Brian Cravens, the book's typographical wizard (and a fellow who came in handy whenever I wished to worry about the book after work at The Little Wagon). To my wife, Ruth Pirsig Wood, who read the galleys with the sharp eye of a scholar and gently pointed out that my diction in some cases was for the birds (feathery tribe?). To Todd Grande, who so brilliantly designed the book and provided its beautiful illustrations. To Grit editors Al Elmer, Michael Rafferty, Joe Subarton, who have encouraged me in my week by week activities on behalf of that newspaper. To photographer Duane Braley who made my wife and I look like Fredric March and Florence Eldrige. And, of course, to publisher Ned Waldman, who spared no expense to achieve a high-quality vehicle to transport my writing efforts to readers.

*—Dave Wood*
*Minneapolis*
*March 1988*

# Contents

# Chapter 1

# How I Got Into This Mess

*The best laid plans of mice
and men aft gang agley.*
—*Robert Burns*

HERE I SIT on a Sunday, faced with another publisher's deadline. This miserable situation was not ever such. My best-laid plans were to reside in the Groves of Academe, clad in tweeds with leather elbow patches, counseling brilliant young students, spend my evenings sipping sherry in an ivy-covered cottage across the street from an ivy-covered college. To that end, I spent four years in college, another six in graduate school, during and after which I taught English literature at six colleges and universities around the Middle West, none of them ivy-covered or sherry saturated, until I left the Groves in 1981 to become a journalist.

I faced different deadlines in those days, all of them more intellectually oriented, none of them as nerve-wracking: A master's thesis due in September 1959, a doctoral dissertation in September 1969 and lots of trips to various registrar's offices to turn in grades for the brilliant young students.

So how did I get myself into my present mess?

Back in 1971, I was coming up for tenure at Augsburg College in Minneapolis, Minn. I had a problem. My field was British literature and that didn't sell very well with students in those troubled days, so my classes were underpopulated and I worried that all those empty desks might be taken into consideration when the committee decided on whether I would stay or leave.

Then opportunity knocked. Augsburg initiated a journalism major and there was no one willing to teach the news-writing course. I volunteered, without portfolio, because I knew that

1

course would fill up with students.

It did and I received tenure. Now I had another problem. Here I was teaching a news-writing course every semester and I had no experience in the world of journalism. In short, I lacked credibility.

Then opportunity knocked again. My wife, Ruth, and I spent our summers on a hobby farm near my hometown, Whitehall, Wis. I had spent my growing-up years there, first with my mother and father on a farm five miles from Whitehall, then with my grandmother and grandfather on Whitehall's Scranton Street after my mother died in 1945 and then with my sister, stepbrother, father and stepmother, whom he married in 1947.

In 1971, Whitehall made national news Ed Goodpaster, to whom this book is dedicated, bought the local weekly newspaper and moved to town. That was news because Goodpaster had been a big-time journalist for years, most recently as deputy Washington bureau chief for Time Magazine.

I met him at a lawn party one night, and he asked me what I did for a living. When I told him, he said, "That must mean you can write English. How would you like to write a weekly column for me?"

I replied that, no, I wasn't certain I could write English. And that yes, I would love to write a weekly column for the Whitehall Times.

So a deal was struck. I was to write three double-spaced pages each week, Ed was to send me $5 per week and I was to achieve credibility as a teacher of journalism at Augsburg College.

Readers seemed to like the column, so at the end of the first year, Ed submitted it for judging by the Wisconsin Press Association. A panel of judges from the state of Washington judged it the best local column in Wisconsin and Ed raised my pay to $10 per week. Boy, thought I, this journalism game isn't very difficult.

I have never won another prize.

After my maiden year, Editor Charles W. Bailey offered me an assignment to write a monthly piece about rural America for the Minneapolis Tribune. This was the Big Time. I approached the assignment with much trepidation and, of course, fell flat on my face. After five outings on the Tribune's editorial page and no response whatever from readers, I was ready to quit or be fired, whichever came first.

And then I wrote them a simple story about simple people having a wonderful time at a not-so-simple church supper. Here it is:

3

# A Church Supper that Smells Fishy

THE NOVEMBER evening is dark and crisp as we pile out of the family Pontiac to partake of the 1950 season's first church supper. Climbing the steps of Pigeon Falls' high-spired white "Upper Church," we catch our last glance at the white moon sitting up there in the blue-black sky and simultaneously catch our first whiff from the church basement — a whiff of lutefisk.

"Uff-da, I hope they got meatballs, too," says Kip, my fourth-grade sister, sounding her oft-to-be-heard culinary pronouncement.

"If they only have lutefisk, keep quiet and fill up on lefse and sugar. You always seem to manage with that on Christmas Eve," Ma counsels.

Through the double doors and into the crowded vestibule we go. A blue-haired lady at the desk sells us mimeographed tagboard tickets proclaiming the

### Pigeon Falls Lutheran Church Supper

*Lutefisk-Lefse-Meatballs-Potatoes*
*Rutabagas, cole slaw, pie*

*Adults $1.25*
*Children $.75*

*Velkommen!*

Murmurs of expectation rustle about the little room.

"It sure is cheaper than serving the stuff at home."

"Yah, and yew keep dat smell outta d'house, tew."

"Yah, but they shouldn't let people eat all they want — some make pigs outta themselves."

"Yah, and lots should know better, tew. Last jeer, I watched dat Nelson from Elk Creek. . ."

"At least we got here early enough this year," Pa says as he lays a five on the table, gets back five tickets and a quarter.

We proceed into the church hall with something less than ascetic reverence. The Rev. Christopherson gives us each a number, that all-important number, but he's so imposing we daren't look at it right in front of him. He asks us in his basso profundo to take seats in a pew and wait for our numbers to be called.

Into the golden-oak pew we slide, a pew rubbed lustrous by more than 60 years of navy-blue pinstripes and black plush overcoats. The yellow-brown overhead chandelier chimneys cast

5

their warm rays on us and we glance at our numbers.

"Five hundred and twenty-seven?" grumbles Pa.

"Five hundred and thirty-one?" whimpers Kip. "Oh, if I'd only gone to Girl Scouts tonight instead."

"Shhh — maybe they're already into the four hundreds," whispers Ma, without much conviction.

*"One hundred ninety through two hundred and nineteen,"* shouts a ruddy fellow framed by the door that leads into the church basement.

"Why an odd number?" asks brother Doug, squirming.

Pa has the answer: "It's old Archie Webb's fault — he usually eats through five or six table settings. Years back he ate 47 meatballs one night up on the hill at Fagernes Church. That tight sonofa. . . "

Doug readjusts his buttocks, wishes he'd gone to La Crosse to watch Gorgeous George wrestle at the auditorium.

I simply salivate. A fatso.

And we all sing. Hymn after hymn after hymn, as people slowly file out and down the basement stairs and as others enter, late, finished with the cursed milking, but swearing they'll come *before* chores next year.

Finally, in the middle of the fourth time through "Living for Jesus," our numbers come up and we proceed, numb-reared, to the basement, Upper Church's Sunday School, its Ladies' Aid-Luther League headquarters and, most important, the best restaurant in the whole world.

The decor isn't much. Yellowed maps of the Holy Land, the Cradle Roll and last week's "S.S. Attendance" deck the hall. Intimacy isn't a strong suit either as we seat ourselves at a papered table with 25 other hungry souls.

But the food! Oh, the food! Here come the red-armed husky ladies with mammoth porcelain bowls of fluffy mashed potatoes, platters of speckled potato lefse, pitchers of melted butter, all emblazoned with the same logo: "Pigeon Falls Creamery Ass." And, finally, lutefisk, all shimmery-flaky, slipping and sliding around on the biggest platters of all.

Chomp, munch, "Pass the butter" — *"Takk"* [thanks]. Clank, munch, chomp.

"Vere are yew from, den?"

"We're from Whitehall."

"Ain't yew got no lutefisk supper in Whitehall no more?"

"No."

"Yew gice down dere gettin' tew *modern*."

General laughter.

"The meatballs got gristle in 'em."

6

"Kip, for God. . . er. . . gosh sakes, would you *shut up*?"

"Yeah, and you can stop *swearing*, too."

Over in the east corner, Archie Webb is tapering off with his third slab of sour cream and raisin pie. If the Mission Society had to depend on customers like old Archie for their revenue, they soon would have to call all the missionaries back from Madagascar. I pass up an offer of pie for one more hunk of that lovely transparent fish, carelessly douse it with too much butter. People look. Pa is embarrassed.

The plump, red-armed ladies are back, urging more food on us, but we all decline with messages for the cooks.

"Da lutefisk vuss *so good* dis jeer!"

"Yah, dis jeer ve soaked it out ourselves — in spring vater and vood ashes."

"Yah, I guess dat's best."

"Yah."

"Yah."

Out into the night we waddle. The first occasion of the church supper season. There'll be others. Elk Creek next week; Fagernes after Thanksgiving. But the first one is always the best, even if you get number 529.

This story, adapted from a real-life experience, won me a shopping bag full of enthusiastic letters and a new lease on life as a journalist, not to mention several invitations to lutefisk suppers from churches across Minnesota, Wisconsin and North Dakota. It has been reprinted in Scandinavian-language publications all over the world, and it is the centerpiece of my after-dinner speaking activities and the most popular chapter in my first book, "Wisconsin Life Trip," published in 1976.

Ed Goodpaster sold the Whitehall Times two years after his arrival in Wisconsin and went back to Washington, D.C., to work for the Washington Post. I stayed at Augsburg and dabbled at free-lance writing until 1981. In that year, I was hired as a feature writer for the Minneapolis Tribune, which would merge with the Minneapolis Star in 1982 to become the Minneapolis Star and Tribune, which in 1987 became Star Tribune, Newspaper of the Twin Cities. Whew! Also in 1981, I received an important phone call. From Ed Goodpaster.

By now, Ed had become publisher of Grit, a 100-year-old national weekly newspaper based in Williamsport, Pa., a newspaper with a vast circulation and a reputation for telling its readers the good news about the world rather than the bad, a newspaper that I had delivered door to door in Whitehall when I was a wee tad.

7

Ed wanted me to write a weekly column for Grit and promised to pay me more than $10 per week. I told him that I already had a good job. Ed said that the Grit assignment wouldn't be too taxing, that I should write the same column for him now as I had in Whitehall.

"It'll be just the same as the old days," said Ed, "and you managed to hold another job then."

So I accepted his challenge, not knowing that it wouldn't "be just the same as the old days," any more than the bowdlerized version of Shakespeare's "A trumpet played in the bed of Caesar" was the same as the Bard's own version: "A strumpet played in the bed of Caesar."

Just before Christmas 1981, I introduced myself to about 800,000 Grit subscribers who live in places as diverse as New York City, N.Y., Effie, Minn., Williston, N.D., and Tucumcari, N.M. A scary prospect to say the least, but I poked it out and sent it in:

~

# The Gift of the Kleppens

IN 1936, the stork delivered me to my parents in the village of Whitehall, where their great-grandparents had settled in the mid-19th century. I have delivered myself from that village again and again, leaving for college, leaving for adulthood, leaving in impatience, leaving for this or that better job. But I always deliver myself back, the village calling me to renew bonds with family and friends or the monuments of my youth.

By 1948, I was doing some delivering of my own, 80 copies of the Winona Republican-Herald. When you do that every evening for five years, you get to know a town and its people. Maybe that's what keeps calling me to the little village that hasn't changed much since those days right after World War II.

Now it's December 1981. The snow drifts down outside the Minneapolis Tribune newsroom, where I work. And my thoughts wander back to the nights when I delivered the Republican-Herald, now called the Daily News for reasons I can't or won't fathom.

As it always does when snowflakes fall on my middle age, one night of all those nights sticks in my memory like angel hair to a Christmas tree: The night that Christmas Eve fell on collection night. The frozen ears, the bent bicycle forks, the deadbeats who left town owing me — all were forgotten as I set out to collect my Yuletide plunder for a year's dogged service.

I remember my route as well as Martin Luther's Small Catechism. First, Johnson's, above the post office, then north on Main Street to "widow's row," the overheated apartments above the bakery, the drugstore, the City Cafe. Usually the hallways smelled of sweeping compound and cabbage, but this blessed night is different. Smells of oyster stew, Norwegian lutefisk and flatbread greet my nostrils as I stride down the oiled-wood hallways.

No tips from the widows doesn't surprise me. But my heart beats faster as I head east across the creek to Gilbertsons' and Bensons'. A quarter. A cookie. Not bad for starters. I hit Scranton Street. Middle class. Solid. My bag fills with boxes of candy, my pockets with quarters. At Grandma and Grandpa Wood's I get a whole dollar they can't afford and a trip to the toilet ("don't forget to put up the seat, Davey!").

And on to Whitehall's Tenderloin, near the Country Club, the area where I put on the face to meet the faces that I meet, sort of a hangdog face, implying that watery gruel awaits me when I return to the chilly little shack where the Wood family is huddling around one dying ember, reading a tattered copy of "A Christmas Carol." The jackpot. Folding money from all three rich people in town.

Then back to reality and the slum hotel just off Main Street. I approach the old Allen Hotel, which leans perilously toward the Texaco station. One family lives there — Oscar Kleppen, his wife and their feeble-minded daughter, Evelyn. The Kleppens hold the distinction of being the town's only welfare family. They're also the only customers on my route who always pay me promptly.

The door opens and Oscar, stone blind, opens the door. The smell of dry rot, dog urine, kerosene, summer sausage and sauerkraut slides out past me into the snowy chill.

"You pay now, Oscar," says the missus, "and I'll get David a cookie."

The soft, anemic cookie sticks to my mitten. The dog pants and rides my pants leg. Oscar feels around in his coin purse. I bite into the cookie and hold the bitten piece in my mouth, ready to spit when I get out the door.

9

"Here's 30 cents. And here's a nickel for Christmas," says Oscar. "Merry Chrith-muth," say I, past the cookie. I back out into the night.

Spit out that cookie? Not on your life. I chew it down and take another bite as I trudge home to huddle near that last ember on our hearth. Merry Christmas, little village. Merry Christmas, world. And God bless us, everyone!

Once the first column appeared, I got letters from all over the country, friendly letters. Because Grit is a "good news" publication, its subscribers want to think the best of everyone, even lower forms of humanity, like writers. People wrote to tell me about their paper routes, about a relative that once lived in Whitehall, a Christmas from their pasts and so I felt better about my prospects.

Nevertheless, the postmarks on the letters indicated to me that I wasn't writing only for readers in the Upper Midwest, but for readers from all over the country, many of whom probably thought that lutefisk was a stringed instrument once manufactured by a now-defunct tire company. So I'd have to set aside the Scandinavian material that I had leaned on in the Tribune editorial page. What would I use for subject matter?

Most certainly, I couldn't respond to news events as many daily columnists do. Grit is more like a magazine than a newspaper and my orders were to write my columns four weeks ahead of time. So by the time my response to a news event appeared in print, its news value had evaporated in a go-go civilization where yesterday's Iranscam is today's bird-cage liner.

Another problem: Most of Grit's readers were so *far away.* When my column appeared in the Whitehall Times, reader response was immediate. On Thursday mornings, people would come up to me in Whitehall's City Cafe, slap me on the back and say, "I enjoyed your write-up in yesterday's Times, the one about lutefisk," or they'd shake their heads sadly, remarking that "You know as much about school board politics as a carp knows about fine dining."

Enough crape-hanging. It's now six years later, I'm still writing my weekly column for Grit. This book is a collection of those columns, each one beginning with a Todd Grande illustration and ending with the year in which it appeared. The columns are not organized chronologically, but by the sources of inspiration — recollections, friends and neighbors, readers, my home town, my relatives and the itch in my belly to keep my mouth full of food. I hope you enjoy reading them and my chronicle of how — with so much help — I manage to crank one out each week.

# Chapter 2

# Remembrance Of Things Past

*"O ft in the stilly night,*
*Ere slumber's chain has bound me,*
*Fond memory brings the light*
*Of other days around me....*

*—Thomas Moore*

IN MY QUEST for column ideas I sometimes get lucky. Just about the time I despair of ever coming up with one more column, I'll look out the window of my office, or look at a pile of overdue work on my desk, or wonder when in hell my vacation will finally roll up to transport me from the workaday world and then my mind will drift off to a more pleasant time. And before I know it I'm recalling such a time in my past that proves to be grist for my column mill. Sometimes a spell of bad weather inspires a story, as was the case for the first column in this chapter. I'm a sucker for changing seasons and so when we get a new one, it usually inspires me to remember something from a season past. Daily life yields story ideas, too, as in the case of the story inspired by watching a colleague eat a Nut Goodie or the day the lights went out in Minnesota or a trip to Anderson's Hardware, just a block from my house.

# An August Night, Long Ago

IT MIGHT have been a rare treat, a party, if the heat had not been so oppressive. At 9 p.m., Grandma Wood announced that everyone was welcome to spend the night on the lawn under the big elm trees. Everyone included us kids, Aunt Alma, my father, my grandpa and the four boarders who made their home at the big old house on Scranton Street. No sense, she said, in sweltering in the rooms upstairs when we could all swelter together on the lawn.

Grandpa got out the lawn chairs, some new metal ones that weighed a ton, some old wooden giants whose paint stuck better to clothes than to wood, and the rickety outfit that suspended a rakish arc of striped canvas, cousin Bill's and my favorite. But it was too hot to fight over, so we made a pact to change off. Grandma spread army blankets out on the parched lawn that wouldn't be green again until next spring. My recently widowed father hooked up an old hammock between two elms, preparing for another restless night of lonesome sleep.

Three of the boarders picked their way down the porch steps made golden by the street light that flickered on the corner. We expected Walter to arrive later, when the taverns closed. He had recently returned from the war and an unsuccessful marriage.

And there we bivouacked in the evening silence, a blaze of stars overhead in the black sky, fireflies gliding lazily in the outer crannies of Mason's house across the street. The little town slept, in T.S. Eliot's words, like a patient etherized on a table. All but its inhabitants. Bill and I knew there wouldn't be much sleeping, which was wonderful, but there wouldn't be any fooling around, either, because all the adults were hoping against hope that Morpheus might penetrate our little band of exhaustion, giving relief and fortification for the difficult day ahead.

We talked fitfully, quietly, almost in a murmur. Grandpa sat there bony-kneed, recalling a summer just like this one, when he was a boy. Was that in 1896, or 1897? Bill and I wondered what it was like to be a boy in 1896 or 1897. Grandma fretted about post-war prices and opined that what this country needed was a darned good depression, like the last one when pork chops were a nickel a pound. Some high school hellions ting-ting-tinged by in a Model A, oblivious to the heat. And to us, camped at the hinges of Hell.

A couple walking by stopped to say hello and wonder when the weather would break, asked the house-coated schoolmarm on the new metal lawn chair when school would begin and then moved on down the street, hand in hand.

13

Grandma disappeared into the house and returned with Kool-Aid for the women, beer for the men, served in cheese-spread glasses. Everyone said that hit the spot. At 11:05, Walter returned from his lonely vigil on a bar stool downtown. He was friendlier than usual, but he disturbed the murmuring etiquette of the evening with tommy-gun bursts of smart talk. Then he was asleep.

By midnight, buttermaker Nelson had dropped off, three hours after his bedtime. My father tossed and turned, the hammock creaked. Soon a z-z-z was heard from Grandpa's edge of camp. Soon, only Billy and I were awake, lying on a prickly army blanket, whispering of school, wondering who would get polio this year. And then we awoke to a dazzling sunrise and the short relief of early morning.

Last night, I thought of that long-ago bivouac, as the air conditioner hummed in our bedroom.

~

# Those Lazy, Crazy Days of Summer

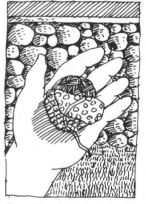

AS I SIT in my stuffy office, work piling up around my earlobes, my thoughts go back to the late 1940s and those first delicious days of summer vacation from grade school.

Back then, in Whitehall, we weren't packed off to summer camp or summer school or sent to Europe to learn about other cultures so that we'd be ready for Harvard when the time came. First, there wasn't enough money for frills like that. Second, my Grandma's only connection with Harvard was a gooey beet dish she made and about which Grandpa always complained.

At 9 a.m., I'd wake up in the big bedroom I shared with my widowed father long after he'd trudged off to work at the feed mill. I'd lie there for a while in my skivvies, cooled by a gentle breeze off the pine trees behind Grandma's clothesline, then dress, pass the closed doors of Grandma's bachelor roomers and go down the L-shaped staircase and into the kitchen for a bowl of puffed rice, shot from guns using very bland gunpowder.

Grandpa could be heard puttering in the old horse barn behind the house, probably making a trellis for the woman he adored. That woman would be snipping chives for the bread-and-butter sandwiches which would make our noon meal, or cooking rhubarb for sauce. Out on Scranton Street, the asphalt was heating up under the steady glare of morning's sun. I knew that by mid-afternoon, when Charlie Schultz came with a block of ice, the air would be shimmering above the asphalt, heat you could see.

What to do for the next 12 hours before bedtime never bothered us kids on Scranton Street.

Maybe we'd sit on my chum Bergie's retaining wall and tear the covers off the scabrous golf balls we'd found a block away in the rough off No. 1 fairway. After the cover was off, we'd carefully pull the thin rubber band until a little rubber ball appeared. A rubber ball full of a mysterious liquid. Bergie said that the liquid was deadly poison and if its rubber container ruptured and you touched the gooey stuff, you'd die. Touch, die. That was it. And that's when Chuck Pederson got out his jackknife to make the initial puncture.

Or maybe Mickey Johnson and I would get a piece of one-inch pine out of Grandpa's scrap box in the old horse barn. We'd saw one end to a point and carve a notch in the other end into which we'd mount a strip of inner tube nailed to a wooden paddle. We'd beg some grocery string from Grandma, tie it to the bow of our new vessel and head across the golf course for the river, then wind up and sail and wind up and sail again the treacherous currents of the Trempealeau until the fire siren atop the old city hall called us to lunch — a lunch called dinner.

During the warm afternoons, before boredom and fear of polio set in around mid-August, we'd swim in the filthy millpond, contract impetigo, get ourselves painted blue by Doc Mac-Cornack, and live to swim again.

In the cool of the evening, after dinner — called supper — we'd sit on the long-unused carriage step by Grandpa's back porch, chew on grass, look up at the stars and wonder aloud about what went on far away from Whitehall, in the world's capitals, including Hollywood, whether or not Chester Morris would make another Boston Blackie movie, if Roy Rogers was really King of the Cowboys and why Istanbul was once called Constantinople.

A month at summer camp might be great and so would a European trip to discover new cultures in preparation for Harvard. But June in Whitehall wasn't bad either. Certainly better than sitting here at my desk, with work up to my earlobes.

～

# Stonehenge was Nothing Like This

THE SUMMER OF 1984 is upon us and I hear romantic balderdash about the old swimmin' hole. Such talk makes my flesh crawl. Old swimmin' holes are not for me. I like the kind of pool that's lined with stainless steel and has more chemicals in it than water.

My present attitude was not ever such. In 1945 Whitehall got a new playground director. His name was Col. Larson. He was an All-American football player in 1939 and he coached all sports at the high school, taught chemistry nine months of the year and then got greedy in summer and took the $300-per-summer playground director-lifeguard job, as if his $1,500-per-year teaching-coaching job wasn't enough to feed, clothe and house a family of four.

Larson was a marvelous man with an infectious enthusiasm for anything he engaged in. One day at the park, as we hammered copper jewelry and tied bowline knots, he announced that the water at the dam was warm enough to open the swimming season. For the first time in its 75-year history, Whitehall was going to offer swimming classes for its youth. I walked home to Grandma's house with images of my swimming the English Channel, having seen "National Velvet" on the previous Sunday. (Remember how Elizabeth Taylor's mother, played by Anne Revere, financed Velvet's running in the National from prize money she earned for swimming the channel before she married Donald Crisp?)

"Swim in that dirty river!?" barked Grandma. Grandpa just smiled. Sixty years earlier, Grandpa left the Baptist church because he didn't want to get baptismally dipped in the muddy waters of the Mighty Trempealeau River.

"Aw, c'mon, Grandma. All the guys are doing it. Col. Larson said that everyone should know how to swim, that it can be a matter of life and death. C'mon . . . "

"Oh, all right," said Grandma. "But you be careful. And don't open your eyes under water."

The next afternoon, we third- and fourth-graders were down at the mill dam in baggy wool swim trunks, wondering why the older boys lingered in the old frame bathhouse, peering through cracks in the boards toward the girls' section.

Col. Larson was a wonderful teacher and within a week he had us dog-paddling about the murky waters below the dam, preparing for the big test of swimming the entire channel in the swiftest part below the spillway. Oh, did we frolic! We did cannonballs off the makeshift diving board. We'd hold our noses and plunge each other under the foamy surface.

After three or four tries, Grandma's stricture was ignored and *I opened my eyes under water!!!*

And what to my wondrous eyes should appear? Long, string-like objects that floated eerily across the floor of the main channel. Blobby, gooey-looking things, like primordial life that crept around at the beginning of time. Grab for one and it would slip away like Glenn Davis, the guy who played halfback for Army. I surfaced and asked Worm Olson, who was older, what those things were.

"Aw, nothing. Just guts from the packing plant upstream."

The next day, I awoke covered with red spots that floated eerily about my tubby little body. Grandma inspected. Impetigo. Off we went to Doc MacCornack, who doled out a big jar of blue ointment. I was ordered to paint myself with it every day until the spots disappeared.

Needless to say, I never got around to swimming the English Channel. But I did walk around Whitehall for a month looking very blue, as blue, in fact, as an English Druid.

~

# Gladly Would She Learn, Teach—And Dance

THE BEAUTIFUL Wife always dreads Parents' Night at the school where she teaches because that's the night folks drop by and ask teachers why they're failing their brilliant kids. "I just don't understand. My Timmy is such a bright boy, all his previous teachers gave him such high grades. And now, well really, a D? You must not be communicating with my Timmy."

In 1942, I matriculated at the one-room school in Larkin Valley, and we didn't have stuff like PTA. We had something that was lots more fun. In Larkin Valley, they called it "Community Club." Parents and students and neighbors and Miss Hanson The Teacher Who Was Beautiful gathered once a month in the yellow brick school that sprouted out of a cornfield. A welcome event, especially along about February or March, when evening radio shows had gone stale and the drafty farmhouses threatened to freeze us to our mohair sofas.

After chores we'd pile into the '33 Pontiac and head for school, a building blessed with electric lights. They cast a warm glow over the oiled floors and the potbellied stove in the corner, as folks hung up their coats in the cloak hall and husky women bustled about in the little kitchen, arranging goodies for after the program.

The program. Barbara Plunkett recited the Gettysburg Address, with barely a mistake. Then it was music time and all but one of seven students, representing six grades, broke into song. That was after Miss Hanson The Teacher Who Was Beautiful had bent down and told Me the Monotone to just move my lips.

Then came a pageant, with Lester Luken playing George Washington I Cannot Tell A Lie, Father. Every once in a while Someone Who Couldn't Hold It slipped out of the little school and made his or her way back to the outdoor privy for relief, but most folks paid attention to what we tots were accomplishing under Miss Hanson's leadership.

No one came to The Teacher Who Was Beautiful and said,

"I just don't understand, my Timmy is such a bright boy, blah blah blah."

When the intellectual portion of the program had been chewed up and spit out, farmers got busy and shoved the rows of desks to one side, over by the lone bookshelf, and Isaac Nelson tuned up his fiddle. Isaac was the neighborhood's Watkins salesman and when he wasn't selling our mothers that wonderful vanilla extract and our fathers horse liniment, he was fiddling. He never charged Community Club for his services. He figured it was good public relations. Besides, the ladies fed him all the heavy cream he could drink. Mrs. Drangstveit would bring him a cup, he'd gurgle it down, wipe off his chin, and saw away again on a tune like "The Arkansas Traveler" while our parents danced.

Out front, by the dried-up lilac bush, a gaggle of non-dancing farmers usually stood in the cold, huddling around a brown bottle full of a mysterious liquid called Four Roses. Probably some kind of perfume. Pa was a dancer and when Ma played out, he screwed up his courage and asked Miss Hanson The Teacher Who Was Beautiful. Darned if she didn't accept and around the floor they whirled.

When Isaac Nelson played out, it was time for lunch. The aroma of strong coffee overwhelmed the Four Roses perfume. There were casseroles, bubbling with noodles and butter, and there were sandwiches of homemade bread and potted meat. And pickles and cake and shimmery Jell-O with real whipped cream skimmed off somebody's can of milk chilling in a spring-cooled milk house.

And then everyone piled into their pre-war cars and went home, with Pa getting *what for* from Ma for dancing with Miss Hanson The Teacher Who Was Beautiful.

∼

## I'm a Man for All Seasons

YESTERDAY in the office there was great wailing and gnashing of teeth, lamentations, threats to take razor blades to wrists in hot baths, longings for early retirement to Sun City or the Sahara.

It was Sept. 26, 1984, in southeastern Minnesota, you see, and the weatherman had said yessireebub, no doubt about it, we'd have frost by morning. So the time of the croaking by frogs was gone and the voice of Jack Frost would be heard in our land.

I sat at my desk and wondered about covering the second wave of pimientos turning red in the garden and whether that old bedspread was big enough to cover four six-foot-tall tomato plants still heavy with fruit and if it would pay to dig up and pot that beautiful basil plant next to the pole beans which had withered weeks ago.

Someone else in the office wondered aloud about the possibility of getting a job on an English-language newspaper in the south of France.

When I got home in the evening, Ruth had already covered the tomatoes. What about the pimientos and basil? It was already

20

brisk so I entered the warmth of the house, ate an omelette stuffed with fresh wild mushrooms we'd picked on the weekend, settled back in the easy chair and decided to let nature take its course. I guess that's because I'm a sucker for the change of season up here in the North Country. I wouldn't have it any other way. So I turned in early, thought about the morrow's pleasant prospect and dropped off to sleep.

The morning smelled and looked great. Coffee cooking in the kitchen, Ruth reading a frost-tipped morning paper. Outside, the towers of Minneapolis aspired above the rosy-fingered dawn. A big green tomato peeked out of our old bedspread, good for mincemeat if it never ripened or maybe for slicing and frying. The pimiento plants were dark green, too dark, and already showed signs of drooping as the sun rose above neighbor Clara Hanson's rooftop. That beautiful basil plant was done for.

Nonetheless, I felt fine as the chill air needled its way through my nostrils too-recently plagued by hay fever. I walked around the garden kicking up frost from clumps of grass and thought of all that autumn meant and means in my life.

It meant tearing ears of corn from rough yellow stalks with Dad husking, then throwing them — thunk-thunk, thunk-thunk — against the high board on the horse-drawn wagon box.

It meant the heart-thumping — boom-boom, boom-boom — as we stole watermelons from sandy plots on black evenings.

It meant making footprints on frosty-white macadam on the way into town for school.

It meant heading for the warmth of home, first walking then running — hoof-hoof, hoof-hoof — after watching a movie called "Dracula," the leaves scuttling across the gloomy night sidewalks of Scranton Street.

Nowadays, it means Saturday afternoon football games, the sun shining down coolly on leather and jersey clacking against leather and jersey.

It means brisk walks around Lake Nokomis with Ruth, talking of plans for the future as another year dies behind us.

It means that soon the garden will be frozen and the parsnips sweet and ready for digging.

I guess I'm a sucker for the change of season.

(*Author's note:* Fun, huh? I was proud of that little column until Grit editor Joe Subarton called from Pennsylvania to tell me that it sounded strangely familiar. And little wonder, for I had already published most of it in 1983 — see *Can we go home again?* below. *C'est la Guerre.*)

∼

# Requiem for a Goldfish

ON JAN. 20, 1982, Mother Nature dumped 17.1 inches of snow on Minneapolis in 24 hours. As the snow piled up around our house, the TV guys in their blow-combed hair and plastic teeth bombarded us endlessly with the news that it was an all-time record for the city. They smiled knowledgeably and told us that "today's precipitation broke the earlier record of 16.2 inches, which fell on Nov. 11th and 12th during the tragic Armistice Day Blizzard of 1940."

The tragic Armistice Day Blizzard of 1940. I was only 4 years old in 1940, but I remember it well and the mere mention of any Armistice Day makes my fingertips tingle. No, I didn't get caught out duck hunting and nearly freeze to death as so many Midwesterners did on that tragic day. And I didn't get stranded on the highway in Pa's 1933 Pontiac, although it was a close call, getting back to our apartment in Eau Claire after a visit to Grandma and Grandpa in Whitehall, just before the highways clogged up.

But my Armistice Day Blizzard of 1940 had its own little tragedy. On the morning after, my two friends and I burrowed our way out of the little apartment building at the foot of Plank Hill and headed for our favorite spot, the tiny concrete fish pond in the back yard. Whatever happened to tiny concrete fish ponds behind little apartment buildings? For that matter, what ever happened to little apartment buildings?

Anyway, the little pond was our favorite spot and we pre-kindergarteners wondered what the blizzard had done to our giant goldfishes and our live, prehistoric version of Kermit the Frog. To our horror, the limpid pool had turned to slush and ice. Susie, Tommy and I wiped our noses across our wooly snowsuit arms and dug in with our mittens. Picking away at the chunks of frozen snow and ice, we discovered to our sadness that our three little fishies would never swim and swim right over any dam.

They were as dead, if you'll pardon the piscatorial expression, as mackerels.

But we kept digging for Kermit and finally discovered him at poolside, his little blue-green body stretched out as if he were taking the sun, his eyes protruding in that startled way of his. And he was stiff as the snotty sleeve on Tommy's snowsuit.

Our fingers tingling, we made our way to Susie's apartment and tearfully told her mother our tale of woe. Clearly, something had to be done. Nowadays, Susie's mother probably would call in the neighborhood psychiatrist to sooth our savaged psyches. But no. "I know!" she said brightly. "We'll make a game of it. We'll have a funeral for the fishies and the froggie. Now let's get busy and dig some graves and find some coffins and make some markers."

So we hunted around and found some shoeboxes, fashioned crosses out of Popsicle sticks, as fishies and froggie lay in state in the back hallway. Once the graves were dug in the drift by the pool, we were ready for the funeral. Neighborhood kids and mothers gathered to mourn and say "Doesn't he look natural?" When we had shoveled the last clod of snow over fishie No. 3, it was time for a last look at Kermit before covering his coffin. We hadn't had so much fun since we put Andrew Johnson's coat on backwards on the way home from Sunday school.

But what was this? Kermit started to twitch. And blink his eyes! Like Lazarus, he had come back from the dead. Murmurs of amazement rippled through the solemn assemblage. Clearly, Kermit had screwed up our funeral.

Tommy looked at Kermit sitting there looking so startled, scratched himself and said, "Let's kill him."

~

# Can We Go Home Again?

LAST OCTOBER I had a week of vacation to burn up, so I went home to Whitehall. Not your conventional vacation in a lakeside cottage or a series of motels near tourist traps. But it was a good vacation. I supped each night at my stepmother's groaning board, I put a roof on the ancestral shed, I watched my nephew play football on a chilly autumn afternoon.

This year we burned up every minute coming to me on our trip to Europe. And so my October will be spent sitting in an office pounding on a video display terminal, progress's answer to a

23

Smith-Corona portable. It's not an altogether pleasant prospect. Already I'm daydreaming of those thoughtless days of youth in Whitehall's October. Back then they didn't seem to be as good as those faraway places with their strange-sounding names we heard calling, calling, us, whenever we could afford to plug a nickel in the jukebox at Pops Mattson's City Cafe. Looking back, October in Whitehall was every bit as good as "April in Portugal."

Here's what was good: (Let's put this in outline form, so we don't get too emotional.)

**1.** Helping Ma carry that dratted kerosene cookstove out of the kitchen once the days cooled off enough to permit firing up the wood cookstove.

**2.** Delivering papers down Scranton Street on chilly evenings, when oak leaves scudded along sidewalks heaving above the roots of elms that had no disease.

**3.** Showering after junior high football practice, coming out of the locker room into the cool night that fell more quickly on each succeeding day, feeling the evening breeze dry up the moisture left by that steamy locker room and its smell of disinfectant and bandages and "red hot" salve.

**4.** Eating crisp side pork, fried potatoes and new Hubbard squash drenched in the butter your dad churned at the creamery, in those golden days before anyone had heard of cholesterol.

**5.** Ambling home from the movie house under a black sky flecked with tiny stars, thinking about Victor Mature trying to strangle old Ethel Barrymore in the second feature, "Moss Rose," then quickening the pace, then running so fast until your heart almost exploded, arriving at the back porch screen door.

**6.** Skulking out into Schansberg's melon patch, with the moon a flat white disc in the sky, wondering if Mr. Schansberg really loaded his shotgun shells with rock salt.

**7.** Idling along the river bed, doing absolutely nothing constructive, on that delicious Friday when your teachers listened to boring speeches at the district convention in Eau Claire, the Big City.

**8.** Crawling between blue-white sheets dried crisp that morning in the sunlight of autumn, hearing rain on the roof, cracking open Lowell Thomas's "With Lawrence in Arabia" for the first time.

**9.** Sensing that anxious, aching void in your stomach when you wondered if one girl with raven tresses would say yes when you invited her to the Freshman Sock Hop after the game with Arcadia. No hurry about asking. You still had two days.

**10.** Tearing ears of corn from rough yellow stalks with Dad

24

husking, then throwing them — thunk-thunk, thunk-thunk — against the high board on the horse-drawn wagon box.

I've run out of Roman numerals, so it's back to the video display terminal and the world of work. (The raven-tressed girl said absolutely not.)

~

## When We Were Privy to an Outhouse

I JUST READ in Grit about the fellow who collects outdoor privies, round privies, privies with vertical siding, that sort of thing. When the Beautiful Wife and I owned our hobby farm in western Wisconsin, we were privy to privies. Our old farm had running water for the cows in the barn, but none for the folks in the house. As the farm's previous owner explained it: "I thought it would be easier carrying water to my kids than to my cows."

That sounded logical to me. And even B.W., who grew up in Chicago, got so she liked the rickety old three-holer out back. It was, after all, a place to read the New Yorker or a Monkey Ward catalog, whichever was handier. And had I subscribed to Grit back then, be assured it would have occupied a prime location in the makeshift magazine rack I nailed to the privy's uninsulated wall. We planted morning glories around the old weather-beaten building and we were set for life, resting easy in the knowledge that we'd never be beholden to plumbers, the Kohler Co., Jacuzzi or anyone.

Then tragedy struck. In 1973, a month after we closed up the farm for the winter, some kids practicing for Halloween sneaked out there and pushed over our privy, which shattered into a million pieces when it hit the ground. It was an act that would go down in the annals of atrocity along with the fire bombing of Dresden and mutilating the Pieta at St. Peter's Basilica in Rome.

So the following summer, we had to rebuild. I announced in my column in the Whitehall Times that our new outhouse

25

wouldn't be some modest little two-holer. Nope, it would be the Taj Mahal of Trempealeau County, Wisconsin. It would be the Petite Trianon of Pigeon Township. I announced plans for a 10-holer, with built-in stereo/television, a wet bar, a fieldstone fireplace and a self-loading catalog-page dispenser that would rough up glossy paper with the flick of a button. There'd also be an auxiliary peach wrapper dispenser for the weeks when B.W. was canning. Our privy along the banks of Pigeon Creek would have a ceiling fan and radiant electric heat built into the bench seat for chilly May mornings.

When folks read that in the paper, they wrote to wish us well and to give us advice based on years of experience glancing at quarter moons around the Midwest. One farmer wrote the following: "If your hired man tends to stay too long in the outhouse, just cut all the holes square and he won't be as likely to sit as long." We ignored that one. You can't get through the New Yorker in just five minutes. Another man wrote and advised us to locate our woodpile on the path between the privy and the house. "That way," he wrote, "You can always pick up an armload of kindling on your way in for breakfast."

Oh, we got lots of advice about corncobs, too, but most of it was stuff not suitable for a family weekly. The best offer we got was from Dave Keenan, the town's Ford dealer who had recently purchased a farmhouse that included a privy his wife, Veronica, wanted out of her sight. My brother Doug hauled it over in his dump truck and set it perfectly on a freshly carved hole. I forgot about building a new Taj Mahal. I painted it white with green trim, planted morning glories around it. I put linoleum on the floor and built a fancy magazine rack. I never got radiant heat installed in the bench, but I did sand it smooth and covered it with bright yellow enamel paint. Then I cut a big window in the west wall, installed a sheet of thick golden plastic from Monkey Ward's. Translucent, of course. And then I rested.

As the warm rays of June sun filtered in through my new window, I sat down and grabbed a 1968 New Yorker and started reading. That's what I call living.

~

# Day of the Long Knife

**W**HEN I GO home to Whitehall, I always run out to Gale Gabriel's beautiful old-fashioned farm in Ervin Coulee. Gale's place was never more beautiful than it was last month, with the leaves on the hills beginning to turn and the windmill creaking a lament of winter to come. Rouen ducks paddled about in the creek below the house, blissfully unaware that my old grade-school buddy had culinary plans for this downy tribe.

Gale raises most of the food he eats, and he'd just returned from a trip to an Amish area called Fly Creek, where a gentle woman had meticulously cleaned a boxful of White Rock roosters and hens that had pecked and strutted about his place until ripe for the executioner's axe.

They were absolutely beautiful, heavy birds, the sort you couldn't buy in a supermarket with a cream can full of silver. Not your 2½-pound fryers with skin the color of a catfish's belly. Nossir. Some of the roosters weighed 8 pounds and fat hung in festoons from their cavities. They were bright yellow and bumpy. And they reminded me of when our family had never seen a turkey in the flesh, much less eaten one, even on Thanksgiving.

The only turkeys we ever saw were in movies at the Pix Theatre, when the father would bring one home for fattening, the kids would fall in love with it, protest the ritual murder, etc., etc. That's because turkeys were a delicacy when I was a kid, an era that fell some time after the Pilgrims ate them on the first Thanksgiving and before every farmer and his brother raised them by the millions. When I was a kid, heavy hens were good enough for us on the farm and for most folks in town who didn't Take On Airs.

Good enough, indeed, I thought, watching Gale develop a hernia as he struggled toward the house with his prize box. The heavies of my memory were absolutely fantastic. In 1943, we gathered at Aunt Doree Johnson's in Black River Falls, because Uncle Leonard was off to the war and she was all alone. We warmed up with a glistening clear chicken broth, cooked from scraps. Then it was time for Doree, my mom and the other sis-

27

ters to mash the potatoes and rutabagas, unmold the cranberries grown a spit away in the Wisconsin bogs, mix the slaw, butter the flaky rolls.

Then Doree got out the big knife and the long, cylindrical sharpener. *Swick-swick-swick*, they said, as Doree expertly swiped them across each other, like a pirate preparing to board a ship of quaking Spaniards. Soon the sage stuffing was revealed and snowy slices of breast and toothsome brown chunks of thigh were spread out before us. And we kids wondered at how anyone could be so dumb as to want the gizzard.

Doree's gravy had a slick of yellow fat across the top, and we poured it over everything on our plates that wasn't sweet. Then we ate and ate and ate until we could eat no more and then we ate some more. Then came coffee and dessert. Pumpkin pie, mincemeat pie with venison in it and Doree's special Mud Puddle Cake, which she'd purposely make to fall, then fill the concave surface with extra chocolate frosting.

After dinner on that Thanksgiving, Doree brought out the Ouija board. We asked it every question we could think of. Except the Big One that was in everyone's heart. When was Uncle Leonard coming home? We were afraid of what the board would answer. Uncle Leonard eventually came back, in 1945, with two Purple Hearts, but as he slogged about in Europe, he missed three Thanksgivings featuring heavy hens, a bird that soon would be replaced by a turkey on every table and two cars in every garage.

~

# My Mother, The Arsonist

IN MID-NOVEMBER Mother Nature shed 11 inches of heavy now on Minneapolis. The cosmic dandruff came down so fast that power lines broke up like so much confetti and there was much lamentation in the land of 10,000 lakes.

Without electricity, people got cold while meat thawed out to such an extent that our frosty state came close to becoming the land of 10,000 steak cookouts. What, moaned younger colleagues, did people do before electricity?

I grew up on a western Wisconsin farm untouched in 1942 by President Roosevelt's Rural Electrification Program. Here, young colleague moaners, is what we did: Pa milked his 20 Guernseys by hand, with only the golden glow of a kerosene lantern to guide him from udder to udder. Ma canned chickens and roasts and vegetables in Mason jars and did our shirts with flatirons heated on a wood cookstove.

When the 12-hour workday was over, we relaxed by our old battery-powered Coronado and chuckled over Jack Benny and his Maxwell or shuddered when someone opened Inner Sanctum's creaking door. And me? I pondered Dick and Jane and Mother and Father, the family that spoke to Spot and Puff and me in monosyllables. Their activities were illuminated by still another kerosene lamp.

It had a graceful chimney, an elegant china fuel tank, shiny brass fittings. And once it threatened to burn our house down.

That was the night Ma decided to discreetly rubberneck on our telephone's party line after a frustrating washday. Ma loved city life and the party line was her link with Western Civilization, actually with Rat Coulee, a tiny valley where she had spent the day wrestling into submission her washer's Briggs and Stratton gas engine.

Usually she rang up Mrs. Olson, Mrs. Johnson, Mrs. Knudtson, Mrs. Hanson or her sister Hazel. But she was younger than the neighbors and sometimes they kept things from her, for her own good, they probably clucked. So sometimes she got that gleam in her eye. (In Adam's fall, we sinned all, saith the primer that preceded Dick and Jane by 200 years.) The gleam usually came when she heard three long rings and a short, Mrs. Anderson's signal. Ma would say, "You keep quiet now, Davey. Otherwise they'll know I'm listening in." I was the only little kid in the coulee. Then she'd step gingerly to the wall phone, put her hand over the speaker, depress the receiver yoke and put receiver to ear.

Oh, and what she heard was usually delicious, especially in winter, when snow kept us from the town library and she'd already read Gene Fowler's "Good Night Sweet Prince" three times.

On the night of the conflagration, I'm fiddling with Dick and Jane and Ma's hearing some real good stuff. About how Tillie Olson's man lost a finger cutting cornstalks, how that Johnson's wife was pregnant again and how maybe Johnson should sleep in the hay barn and how that Knudtson girl, the fast one, you know, how she lives in Minneapolis now and how only the Lord knows what she's up to in that fleshpot.

And then I notice that the lamp's chimney is smoking up. So I tug on Ma's dress to apprise her of imminent disaster and she swipes at me blindly with the hand that should have been cupped over the speaker. I tug again and she grabs a handful of my forelock and shakes. Now flame shoots out of the chimney, perilously close to the sheer window curtains.

*"Ma!!! The lamp's on fire!!!"*

Ma drops the receiver, races into the living room where the curtain is merrily crackling away. She drags it out and onto a snowdrift where the flame sizzles and pops and dies out. And then she sits down, elbows on the oil-clothed kitchen table, and cries.

Back in the living room, the receiver swings back and forth freely on its cord. Putting my ear close, I hear Mrs. Anderson's voice crackle over Alexander Graham Bell's gift to Rat Coulee: "Yah, I guess when she got to Minneapolis, she got a job as a waitress, in a night club, would you believe. ... "

And that, young moaning colleagues, is what we did before electricity.

~

## The Consarned Human Race

"**IT'S 20 BELOW** zero, Davey," said Grandma, as she choked my fat little cheeks purple, adjusting the scarf at my neck, then made secure the string of yarn that ran along my shoulders, down my sleeves to left and right mittens. "So when you get cold, be sure to come in and warm up."

She pointed an arthritic index finger at me, riveted my attention with an icy blue-eyed stare and concluded her sermon: "And whatever you do, don't stick your tongue on the pump handle!"

Stick my tongue on the pump handle? That pump had stood in the back yard for as long as I or my father could remember. I'd pumped it furiously in summer and stuck my head under the water that gushed out its spout. Or I'd pretended it was a Flash Gordon rocket launcher. Or pried up a board and peered down into the masonry and hollered something, then waited for the well to holler back. But stick my tongue on its handle? No way.

So out I trudged into the back yard and stuck my tongue on the pump handle.

My little pink protuberance stuck fast and in a panic I jerked back leaving a patch of myself on old friend pump. Then I ran in to warm up and bleed all over the kitchen sink. For weeks my tongue looked like an aerial photo of erosion in the Cumberland Gap.

Thanks for the warning, Grandma.

This childhood episode demonstrates what the Holy Bible and Mark Twain have been warning us about for centuries: Man is about as perverse a creature as you'll find in the solar system. Tell him not to do something and however unappealing the deed, he'll be certain to do it. God told Adam and Eve that they could lie around and eat pomegranates in the Garden of Eden till seeds ran out their ears. Or any other fruit for that matter. Except from that one little tree. And what did they do? They went right over and took a bite. Since those two traveled east of Eden, it's been the same old story.

Grandma was also big on ears. "Don't ever put anything in your ears smaller than your elbow." Then she'd point the arthritic finger: "And whatever you do, don't stick beans in them." Then I'd head for the pantry.

Other warnings:

"When you're at school, don't eat library paste."

"When you're on summer vacation, don't smoke corn silk."

"Now that you're back from the hospital and your appendix scar is healing, don't pick up that shotput and try to throw it!"

"Don't go swimming in that scum-covered river this time of year or you'll get impetigo." (See earlier column, *Stonehenge Was Nothing Like This.*)

Perhaps the most shocking experience of my childhood came when Pa bought his first electric fencing unit. World War II had made barbed wire hard to come by, so Pa set up a single electrified wire around the barnyard to keep three or four crazy young heifers from wandering across five counties. Right off, one of the heifers decided to do battle with the new contraption. She took a run and when her bovine head touched the wire, she backed tail over teakettle into a juicy manure pile by the barn door.

Pa looked at me with all his wisdom and said, "Davey, that should be a lesson to you." Then, pointing his calloused index finger at me, delivered himself of the sermon's conclusion: "And whatever you do, don't wee-wee on that wire!"

Thanks for the warning, Pa.

～

# *Cleanliness Is Next to Godliness*

**T**HESE DAYS, I'm so clean I squeak. I've been sort of clean for several years, but never enough to make me squeak. For years, I've taken a daily bath and so I guess that, up until recently, you'd call me sort of average clean. I began to squeak three weeks ago, when piles of snow piled up on Minneapolis sidewalks, making my daily constitutional uncomfortable if not impossible. I felt the need for exercise, so I joined the YMCA and now I swim every morning before going to work.

They won't let you into the pool at the Y unless you take a hot, soapy shower first. So I shower at 7 a.m., jump into the pool at 7:05, swim until 7:30, then go into the sauna until 7:45, emerge looking like a fat lobster. Then back into the shower for five minutes to wash away my rosy hue and then to work at 8. I work until 5, then come home and take a bath to wash away my nerve-inspired effluvia. That's a lot of water passing over my rotund frame every day. And that's why I squeak. In three weeks my skin has turned from a very pale tan to bluish white, the kind of bluish white you see on the belly of a channel catfish pulled out of the Mississippi in springtime.

I was not always squeaky clean.

When I was a kid, growing up in Rat Coulee, County of Trempealeau, State of Wisconsin, I was covered with scales six days of the week. I suspect there are a few Grit readers out there who know what I mean. Maybe half a million or so — the half-million Grit readers who grew up on farms without benefit of indoor "facilities." City folks had bathtubs, but we didn't. What we had was a sink in the kitchen with a slop pail underneath. I washed my face and my hands with a big bar of stinky Lifebuoy on Monday, Tuesday, Wednesday, Thursday, Friday and Sunday. But under my clothes were scales. Not fish scales, dirt scales. I don't think I ever smelled, but how am I to compare, because none of the other farm kids who sat next to the potbellied stove in the one-room schoolhouse lived in homes with benefit of indoor facilities. Come to think of it, my mother took sponge baths every day and she smelled a lot better than the men of the family. Maybe I did smell.

Then came Saturday. My mother set up the big washtub in the summer kitchen where she cleaned eggs. I was ordered to strip. As I stood there in the altogether, shivering next to the frosty window to the porch, she poured steaming water from the wood cookstove reservoir into the galvanized tub. When it was one-third full, I stuck a scaly toe in: *whoof! hot!!!*

"Don't lollygag around until the water gets cold," she admonished, plopping a hunk of pink Lifebuoy into the steaming cauldron. So as my body took on the hue of a skinny lobster, I lathered up without much enthusiasm while mother went back into the kitchen to tune into "Your Hit Parade." As Frank Sinatra's young voice drifted in from the Coronado on the end table, I washed a little here, a little there, until the water turned just warmish and began to resemble the backwaters of the Trempealeau River during dog days.

Then mother would check behind my ears, toss me a towel, which I used to wipe off the sludge before it froze to my frame. Then it was my father's turn and he'd howl a bit as he lowered himself into a fresh batch of $H_2O$ from the reservoir. I've always wondered what he looked like, all 6-feet, 1-inch of him sitting in that galvanized tub. But I wasn't allowed to look, because that wasn't proper.

Too bad they didn't have a YMCA in Rat Coulee, where Sunday mornings found huge gray ice cubes just beyond our porch.

∼

# Quarantine!

WHATEVER HAPPENED to scarlet fever and all those other diseases that caused red quarantine signs to sprout on houses along Scranton Street in those long-gone springs of my youth?

I suppose we must be thankful for the wonders of modern communicable-disease control systems. But I still look back on those red and black signs that kept one out of school for up to four weeks. Think of it. Four whole weeks! Sure, sure, mumps could be miserable and chicken pox chilling. But remember all the attention you got?

I got mumps during the spring of third grade, and Aunt Floy Harlow, with whom I was living after my mother's death, plied me with soothing custards and presented me with my all-time favorite comic book. It was about an inch thick. A Classic Comic rendition of the Bible. I still remember Joseph and his coat of many colors, in color. Aunt Wylis gave me a xylophone and I plinked away at that in my bedroom as my jowls receded. (These days they're back up there with the jowliest.)

The only person who didn't give me a present was my recently widowed father. No, he wasn't cruel. Seems I'd spent a weekend with him and given him the mumps. He was 35 years old at the time and he stayed in bed at Grandma Wood's, too delirious to play a xylophone, for several weeks. Too bad, dad.

Measles were a snap in fourth grade. But the doctor warned me that I shouldn't read, lest I go blind in later life. That was a restriction I didn't mind at all. As my geography and science textbooks gathered dust on the night stand, I listened all morning to stuff like the "The Transcribed Adventures of Judy and Jane," "Pepper Young's Family," "Our Own Ma Perkins." At night, there was "Lux Radio Theatre," "Inner Sanctum" and you know the rest. I've been weak in geography and science ever since and I got bifocals when I was 21, but it was worth it. I've always been strong on Shuffles and Willie at Ma's lumber yard and I can still do the opening of "Our Gal Sunday": "Can this girl from a mining town in the West find happiness with the wealthy and titled Englishman, Lord Henry Brinthrop?" See?

But the very best disease I ever had was scarlet fever. That

35

came in the spring of fifth grade. A terrible epidemic. All the kids along Scranton Street got it at about the same time. And Doc MacCornack came and ordered the red-and-black signs up. Four weeks. It was a warm spring and jonquils pushed themselves through the moist soil along the stone foundation of the Wood estate. I was sick for all of five days and then felt fit as a Stradivarius. So did Bergie and Mickey and Worm Olson and all my buddies.

So when no one was looking, we'd venture out to smell the grass and mud and hear the sounds of spring, see Wisconsin's state bird, the robin, hopping around bored and arrogant as usual. Of course there was one minor problem with all these quarantine vacations. You couldn't leave your own yard. So we'd stand on our own turf and shout insults and jokes at each other. Bergie would get really witty and call me "dumbhead" and I'd rejoin with something equally sharp, like "you're a jerk." And then we sailed paper planes at each other, torn out of our pulp paper tablets. No use doing the homework. We had two weeks, no, I guess it's one, no, it's just two days now until we'll return to Whitehall Memorial School. Jeepers. We'll do it tomorrow.

And of course there was catch to play. Doc Mac never said the ball was quarantined. Or did he? Well, never mind. And so that's how it went in that disease-plagued yesteryear, after the spots disappeared and the voice of the turtle was heard in our land.

~

# Trade You A Nut Goodie
# For An Almond Joy

GOSH HOW I long for those simpler times when three nights a week I squiggled into a seat in the seventh row of the Pix Theatre in Whitehall for a look at Hopalong Cassidy or Gene Autry or Lash LaRue or even Roy Rogers, who wasn't really the King of the Cowboys. (It was as plain as the nose on my face that Gene was).

After that there'd be Chester Morris as Boston Blackie, with Richard Lane as the stupid police inspector who was always getting himself locked in hotel closets so Blackie could be free to find the crook. Or William Powell and Myrna Loy in one of the Thin Man movies. What a class act they were!

We've got cable TV now and so we can watch those wonderful old movies. But somehow it isn't the same. I've wondered why ever since we subscribed to cable. And now I know.

Wanna know how I know? Here's how: At my office, I sit about 15 feet from Lee Svitak Dean, who writes about food for the Minneapolis newspaper. She's way too young to remember Gene or Lash or Hoppy, but she's got this father, who is very important to the way our office operates. His name is Don Svitak and he's vice president of operations for Pearson Candy Co. in Minneapolis.

And so every once in awhile his daughter shows up at the office with free samples. A week or so back she showed up with a Pearson Salted Nut Roll. This wasn't your ordinary Pearson Salted Nut Roll. This had been fabricated the day before. And it weighed 25 pounds.

A colleague took a butcher knife and whacked through the fresh salted peanuts to reveal a creamy white nougat interior. I'm on a diet, as usual, and so I stayed away all morning. By noon — I'm not lying — I could *smell* that giant candy bar. After a sumptuous lunch of Ry-Krisp and cottage cheese, I crept over to the table and sliced off a hunk and popped it in my mouth.

*Holy Moley, Captain Marvel!* I figured out why watching Boston Blackie at home wasn't the same as it was at the Pix Theatre. We don't have any Salted Nut Rolls at home! So I can't squiggle into my easy chair and wait for the sun to go down, when I can tear open the wrapper, then eat each salted peanut individually, then nibble into the nougat until it's gone by the fourth reel.

See, Pearson Salted Nut Rolls were a blessing to us kids from the wrong side of the tracks. The rich kids always walked into the Pix, bought a box of popcorn *and* a candy bar. But those of us who only got 20 cents for the movies, ended up with 8 cents change from the box office. Popcorn cost a dime, so that was out. Then we discovered the nut roll. Start with the salty part, move on to the sweet. A perfect, although saline, solution.

And then came high school and a 35 cent tariff at the box office. That ruined a 50-cent piece because by that time popcorn had gone up to 15 cents, so us urchins turned to the ever-popular Nut Goodie, a sinful confection with a maple-cream filling covered with nuts covered with milk chocolate. The lights went down, we tore open the red, white and green wrapper, nibbled around the beveled edges slowly and waited for the second feature before tearing into the maple cream.

Covered with nuts. Guess who makes Nut Goodies? You got it, Pearson Candy Co. I wonder if I could persuade my colleague to persuade her father to fabricate a 25-pound Nut Goodie, one that would last through about four weeks of cable TV watching. C'mon Hoppy, catch that villain played by Roy Barcroft.

~

# Mine Enemy Chews Tobacco

**D**EAR ARLIE EVERSON:
I should have confessed this to you and Walter years ago. But I kept putting it off and putting it off. Finally, I stored it away in my subconscious and didn't think about it for many years. Just now I'm smoking a cigar and thinking about my days in the tobacco industry. So now I have to tell you, Arlie. I only wish your husband, Walter, were still around to hear my confession and offer forgiveness. It all began about 35 summers ago, when you were newlyweds, farming the old Lake Farm near Coral City. If memory serves, Pa and Walter talked over my lack of gainful employment that summer. After all, I was 12 years old and every day of idleness meant I was getting closer and closer to the jungle jim at the Devil's playground. So Pa and Walter struck a deal. Walter would hire me to pick tobacco worms.

The job sounded sort of ishy to a town kid from a metropolis like Whitehall. Picking tobacco worms. Aargh! What did tobacco worms look like? Were they like angle worms? That wouldn't be so bad. Or were they like grubworms? That would be bad. My questions were meaningless because Pa was determined that I didn't read Captain Marvel comics the whole summer. So on a Monday morning, I rode my Hawthorne out to your farm and Walter introduced me to the world of the tobacco worm.

We walked out into the patch of waist-high, lush-green tobacco. Walter said, "Listen now, Davey, for a noise. You hear that noise and you lift up a tobacco leaf and there'll be a worm." We walked down a row and I heard lots of noise, *loud* noise that sounded like clickety-clickety-click as fast as you could say it. But a worm certainly couldn't make a noise like that.

"Hear that, Davey?" asked Walter. "That clickety-clickety-click?"

"Yup. I hear it, but that can't. . . . "

"That's a tobacco worm under that leaf right there. And it's eating my tobacco."

(Omigod!)

Walter lifted the leaf, Arlie, and I about fainted when I saw my first tobacco worm. It was bright green and had regularly spaced dents around its dime-sized circumference, making it look sort of like an Italian salami covered with green mold. My first worm was about four inches long. That was bad enough. What really got me was the spike sticking out of its head, like a tiny unicorn horn. Walter grabbed the worm by its horn and pulled. R-r-r-i-i-p! said the worm's several feet as they parted company with the plant. Walter plopped the worm in a Mason jar half full of kerosene, then handed the container to me.

"You just walk up and down the row. When you hear that chewing, pick the worm and throw it in the jar. I'll pay you a penny for every worm you pick. Just count 'em up at the end of the day." .

A penny a worm, count 'em up. Fear struck out, and larceny stepped up to the home plate of my heart. I made my way up and down the rows, in the hot June sun. Clickety-clickety-click. Raise leaf. R-r-r-i-i-p! You served me a wonderful lunch, Arlie, and back I went into the field. I finished off at 4 p.m. Walter was still out haying, so I crept behind the silo.

And then, Arlie, I did It. I picked each worm out of the kerosene. And I tore each in half. One-two, three-four, four cents for two worms, green tobacco juice oozing out of each rupture. After I'd toted up 198 pieces for 99 worms, I kicked the mess into some tall grass by the silo, told you Walter owed me $1.98 and rode back into town. Walter paid me without a question. Since then, only God knows how much this evil deed untold has goofed up my psyche. Now you know, Arlie, all Grit readers know, and I can walk in the sun once more, with my head held high. After I pay you 99 cents. Regards, Dave.

~

# *Three Tenpenny Nails, Please*

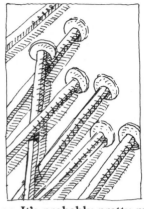

**S**OME THINGS change and some thing stay the same. And I like the latter lots better than the former.

We live in a south Minneapolis neighborhood that was developed in the '20s. It's a modest area of stucco homes with tile roofs looked down upon by old elms. Two blocks from our house, there's an old-fashioned shopping area with a grocery store, a movie theater, a bank, all the things you need to keep body and soul together. It's probably pretty much the way it was back in 1924, when our house was built, except for neon and plastic signs and plastic food on the freezer shelves of Dealer's Market. It's a great little corner, because we can walk over whenever our body or our soul starts falling apart.

But some places are better than others. You take the drug store. Every time I toddle over to get a new bottle of blood pressure pills, my pressure shoots up. Not because it's a bad drug store. It isn't. It's just not like the one I remember from my childhood. Fortun's on Main Street in Whitehall was your basic drug store. Roy Fortun sold drugs and darned little else. Oh, sure, he had cigars, good ones too, the kind the banker bought. And he had a soda fountain with a soda maker that shot a tiny laser-like stream that might have cut a hole in the bottom of the glass that held the lime and phosphate you had just ordered.

When you went to Fortun's for your grandma, you spent the nickel she gave you at the fountain first, lingered as long as you could, picked up the pills from Roy. On your way out you gave the punk and spark cigar lighter a whack, it sputtered *z-z-z-z* and Roy Fortun sputtered ?&@*!?$#! And then you beat it for home.

The drug store in our neighborhood sells drugs, too, but as you walk in, you wonder if that's not just a sideline. Our drugstore sells no-name pork and beans, Vienna sausages made by a packing plant you've never heard of, huge jars of dry-roasted peanuts. It sells fake brass wastebaskets and earrings that turn your ears green. It sells trashy magazines, kitchen utensils and crystal glassware made of plastic.

Up by the pharmacist's counter, there's a display of tiny magnets posing as tiny vegetables and fruit. Something with

41

which to stick reminders onto the refrigerator door.

There's nothing wrong with those little magnets. But I miss Roy Fortun's cigar lighter.

Across the street is the Our Own Hardware Store, operated by Sven Anderson as if he were in a time warp. Oh, sure, Sven carries the new glues and the new tools and stuff I wouldn't be without. But he's into hardware, by golly, and it's very difficult to find a snowcone or breakdance shinguards in his store. Andy will repair your storm windows and your lawn mowers and your snow blowers. He'll sell you one stove bolt or five wood screws, so you don't have to buy a plastic bag of them.

You want three tenpenny spikes to anchor a trellis? You can buy three of them and Sven or his clerks will be just as polite to you as they were to the fellow who just walked out with a self-starting lawn mower.

In lots of neighborhoods like ours, the small stores that have been there for half a century or more are dying out. Folks are going to the suburban centers because some things cost two cents less. Somehow Sven Anderson is always busy, because the Hardware-Rama in Magicdale Mall won't sell you three tenpenny nails or fix your floor lamp — even if they know how.

~

# Chapter 3

# Friends and Neighbors

*T*he vulgar estimate friends by the advantage
to be derived of them.

*—Ovid*

I'M NOT EXACTLY your Richard Harding Davis, Richard
Halliburton or Lowell Thomas sort of journalist. I've never
been out on the desert with Lawrence of Arabia, preferring
instead to drink a beer at the corner bar with Lawrence of the
Knutsons. And I always try to adhere to the most important rule
for writers: Write about what you know about. So my Grit columns are not the stuff of which Steven Spielberg films are made.
Can you imagine a movie called "Indiana Wood and the Temple
of Lutefisk"?

The only thing I know about is what I do and what I do is
live at home, work at the office and go to lunch. Once a year I
take a vacation. In this chapter, you'll read columns inspired by
my neighborhood in south Minneapolis, by my daily luncheon
partners at The Little Wagon, a downtown saloon where a band I
play in performs on Tuesday nights — performs atrocities on
perfectly good music, that is. And by wonderful people my wife
and I have met on our vacations.

# A Rooftop Idyll

I SAT OUT on our back porch of an evening recently, gazed across the back alley to the Moores' residence on 10th Avenue. I looked up at the roofline of the big two-story dwelling and wished I were there.

It was 8 p.m., May 1. Two pompous robins busily looked for the seeds I'd just planted. The temperature was balmy and the buds on the elms were finally springing forth. The lawns shone green in the evening sunlight, recalling the poet Richard Eberhart: "This fevers me, this sun on green, on green glowing this young Spring."

Up on the Moores' roof, above the arrival of spring, halfway to the stars that would appear in an hour or so, lay the Moore boy and his buddy Michael, who lives next door. They're both about 14; one is black, one is white, and they're always together, discovering the joys and sorrows of adolescence. They shoot baskets, tease the girls at the school bus stop, envy an older kid on the block who constantly tunes his race car and, I'd guess, just enjoy the heck out of life.

How they got up on that steep roof, under those 60-year-old elms, is anybody's guess. But you can bet it wasn't with the aid or approval of their parents. There they lay, forearms crossed under their chins, savoring the delicious detachment of undetected sin. Occasionally they spoke softly, or suppressed a giggle, or bounced around, readjusting their gangly frames to the hard, gritty surface of the asphalt roof.

I sat on the porch, my old bones and flabby muscles screaming with pain after a few hours in the garden. And I wished I were up there, wished I were *able* to get up there, relishing the joys and sorrows of adolescence, enjoying the heck out of life. But there I was, 46 going on 90, earthbound and sore. So I sat and wondered what they might be talking about, the boy with curly black hair, the boy with the mop of straight flaxen stuff always in his eyes.

Most certainly there was talk of school, the imminent three-month vacation and trips to nearby Lake Nokomis. Most certainly there was talk of when will your folks be home and should we get down before we're caught. And, if my memory serves me, there was talk of girls, girls, girls.

The birds chattered, punctuating an evening that breathed deeply, as if in sleep. An occasional car passed the Moore residence, but no motorcycles roared down the alley to break the magic of the first pleasant evening since the snow began to fall last November. The boys rolled around and perched their bony bottoms on the roof peak and looked down at me, wondering if I'd fix them with a baleful gaze. They needn't have worried. Adults merely talk about how wonderful spring evenings are. But adolescents live those evenings, soak them into their very beings not knowing intellectually how important they are, but enjoying them in their pure naturalness. So I wasn't about to interrupt their reverie as they sat for half an hour without saying a word.

A yellow Ford pulled into the alley. It was Nell, the black fellow's mother. A wonderful woman and a strict disciplinarian. The sound of six cylinders sent the boys hunkering down on the other side of the roof, out of Nell's sight. She got out of the yellow Ford. Hi, Dave, isn't this evening wonderful? Hi, Nell, it certainly is and about time, wouldn't you say?

As we spoke, I shot a sidelong glance halfway to the stars and two heads appeared on the Moores' roof line. Nell entered her house. Then the boys waved at me and although it was too far away to tell, I think they smiled at the fat old man sitting on his back porch, never realizing he wanted to be up there with them.

~

# The Squaretable Wits Go Fishing

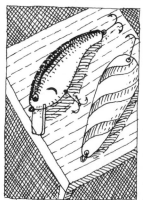

**M**OST NOONS of the workweek, I lunch with this bunch of downtowners who are usually Fine Fellows. We eat, we solve the problems of the world, we lie, and we tell jokes, not as funny as those cracked at the Algonquin Hotel's famous Roundtable back in the '20s. So we call ourselves the Squaretable Wits. Generally, we're good at what we do. Most of us can pack away a day's supply of calories in that short hour without even burping. Most of us can read, so we know what's going on and thus have short, simple answers to the Most Pressing Problems in the World. Lying is second nature to all of us. Most of our jokes function on a High Level of Good Taste, with the exception of those by Dick Caldwell. (More about him in the next column.)

But when fishermen in the group decide to go on a trip, then the little world of The Little Wagon restaurant spins out of orbit, leaving those of us who think Izaak Walton was the grandpa on that TV show twirling our thumbs to fend off terminal boredom.

Last spring, the anglers started at it. A trip to Crow Lake in Canada. They'd rent a big recreational vehicle and it would be a Really Good Time. Free lodging was available, etc., etc. For the next two weeks, those fishermen ate listlessly, forgot the problems of the world, never told a lie and looked at those of us who did as if we'd just kicked an aging auntie. They had Serious Matters to discuss. Rod discussions. Reel discussions. Twelve-pound test line discussions. Ice cooler discussions. How many outboards to bring discussions and would there be room in the boat they were towing to bring back all the fish discussions.

When that was over, they discussed the sociology of present-day Canadian piscatorial habitats.

And on the seventh day they rested.

After that, they got down to brass tacks: Provisions. For an entire lunch hour, they pored over long check lists of foods, beverages, extra shoelaces, deodorant, condiments, fresh fruit, canned fruit, dried fruit, first aid kits. Finally, the budget was struck and all seven Fine Fellows agreed to throw in $200 for the trip. And two days later, they left for five glorious days of casting, catching and camaraderie.

And those of us who remained in Minneapolis got back to our normal noon at The Little Wagon. We ate too much with gusto. We solved the world's problems. We joked. We lied. And then we thanked the Big Tenderfoot in the Sky for our respite from those brutal torturers of the Finny Tribe, having all that fun, catching all those fish.

Then, like hunters and fishers since prehistoric times, the piscatorians returned from their food-finding expedition. They filed in to The Little Wagon and sat down at their appointed places. Those of us who had stayed behind to keep the fire pretended we were glad to see them. But we knew that we'd spend another week hearing about how the 12-pound test line snapped, about the pickerel as big as a miniature submarine and how Phil lost his specs in Crow Lake.

"How'd it go?" we asked in hollow tones. "Bring any fish for us?" "How was the weather?" The fellows looked as if they'd been standing in 38-degree water for five days — in hip boots that were too short. The weather was cold, they said. The fish weren't biting, they said. But Dick Caldwell caught one, they said. One!? One. And they ate it on the night before returning. Most figured that meal cost $280 per pound. Caldwell said the fish weighed more than that, that the meal cost only $200 a pound. And then they all ordered ribeye steaks from Annabelle the Waitress. At $5 per pound.

~

# The Three-Legged Pig

I LIKE A JOKE as well as the next man, but too much is too much. When a fellow starts telling stories that make fun of pigs, then he's attacked one of my sacred cows, er, sacred pigs, and he's got me hopping mad. See, I've liked pigs since I was a kid growing up on a farm and Pa kept a couple to fatten with a little corn and the contents of our slop pail. Pa always told me that a pig was smart, a pig would never lie in manure if you gave that pig half a chance. Pa said a pig was about as clean as an animal could be and that a pig only laid in the mud because that beautiful pink pig skin didn't have any pores.

Oh, sure, Ma eventually had her way with those pigs and that wasn't too pleasant when you heard them squeal under the knife. But she fixed it so they all achieved their own special immortality. Ma like to tear the tenderloin out of a slab of pork chops right after butchering and fry it on the spot. (Pa said her side of the family never had much discipline.) Later, their cracklings graced our fried potatoes all winter. Their side pork sizzled and snapped in the skillet of a frosty night. And the pork chops, even without the tenderloin, served us well, with a little milk gravy on the side.

So you can imagine how I get my bristles up when someone tells a story at the expense of a pig.

It happened at lunch today, when my ex-friend Dick Caldwell got going on a pig story. I expected more from Mr. Caldwell, for normally he's a man of some wit, having recently finished a manuscript entitled "The Flying Chef," which tells of a fellow who flies around the world in a plane cooking meals for people. As yet, it hasn't been accepted for publication and I've sympathized with Caldwell. But after so-and-so's noontime performance, I'm beginning to wonder if publishers don't have some brains after all.

Former friend Caldwell polished off a pork tenderloin sandwich and told the following tale:

"Seems this feed salesman called on a farmer and as he was talking noticed a pig on the porch. And the pig had a wooden leg, left rear quarter. The salesman said, 'That's some pig, how'd it ever get a wooden leg?' 'Well,' the farmer said, 'that pig's an exceptional pig. Just three years ago, I was plowing up yonder on that hilly 40 and the John Deere tipped over and pinned me. I figured I was a goner, but darned if that pig didn't show up. He started rooting around with his snout and damned if he didn't manage to upend the John Deere. I slid out from under and today my old body is just as good as new.

" 'And that ain't all. Just two summers ago, we were swimming in the pond in the pasture. My youngest son, Lyle, he swam out into the middle and got a cramp. Well, none of the rest of us can swim, but sure enough that pig, he came running up, dove into the pond, swam out and dragged little Lyle right back to us and then gave him artificial respiration. Lyle, he'll be in fifth grade next year.

" 'And last year, well my-oh-my. We was all fast asleep and had ourselves a chimney fire. The house was a blazing inferno and we'd have been sprouting wings about now if it hadn't been for that blamed pig. He got out of his pen and dragged us all to safety. Some pig, I'd say.'

" 'Sure, sure,' said the feed salesman. 'But you still haven't told me why that pig has a wooden leg.'

" 'Well,' the farmer said, 'You take an exceptional pig like that, and you sure don't want to eat him all at once!' "

~

# Caldwell Redux

A FEW DAYS AGO, Squaretable Wits lingered long over coffee as Dick Caldwell spun a tale of Samuel Pepys, the 17th-century British diarist.

"David, do you know that Pepys was aboard the ship that brought Charles II back to England from exile in France?"

"Gee, no, Dick, I didn't."

"Did you know he was a Cambridge classmate of the poet John Dryden, that he was for a time president of the Royal Society and a good friend of Sir Isaac Newton and the architect Christopher Wren?"

"No, I guess that slipped by me."

"Pepys' family was Huguenot and he survived a gallstone operation at the age of 25, went to work for the government and ended up as secretary to the admiralty and a member of Parliament."

"Gee, Dick, that's really interesting."

"You know, Dave, the diary, which he wrote in code, runs to more than a million and a half words. It provides a wonderful account of life in the late 17th century and events like the Great Plague of the 1660s."

"I wouldn't doubt that a bit, Dick. More coffee?"

Caldwell looked at me in that probing journalist's way of his and said this:

"Wood, doesn't this strike you as a rather curious conversation?"

"Curious?" I said. "Why curious?"

"Well," said Caldwell. "You have a doctorate in 17th- and 18th-century British literature, right?"

"Yes, that's right."

"And you've read from the diaries of Samuel Pepys?"

"Yes, I've read the abridged version."

"And me," said Caldwell, "I studied journalism at college, no English."

"Yes, that's right."

"And here," said Caldwell, "I sit for half an hour lecturing you on Samuel Pepys and his 17th-century diaries. You're supposed to be a scholar. Aren't you curious about how I know all this stuff when you apparently don't?"

"Gee," said I, "I guess I thought it was because you were really smart."

"Sure, sure, I'm smart. But not that smart. I read all that stuff I told you about Pepys out of a book my father-in-law gave me."

"Your father-in-law gave you a book about Samuel Pepys? That's a rather curious present."

"No, no, not about Pepys. It's a book put out by the Reader's Digest and it's called 'Stories Behind Everyday Things.' It's alphabetized and I read one letter a night before falling asleep. I found Pepys in the D section, under 'Diary.' "

Finally, we went back to work, Dick promising to lend me the book as soon as he'd fallen asleep on the Z section. And I wondered why I ever spent 10 years getting that dratted Ph.D. when I could have gotten as much out of reading myself to sleep.

Last week, he brought me the book. I've read through the C's. This is not for bedtime. But if we only had a privy, I'd be in Seventh Heaven.

(*Author's note:* Some of you might think I'm making too much of Caldwell, but if you were ready for a long vacation and a Grit deadline was staring at you, wouldn't you have strung out the "Stories Behind Everyday Things" for at least one more week? You wouldn't have? Well, I did, and here it is.)

~

# Getting Indigestion With
# the Reader's Digest

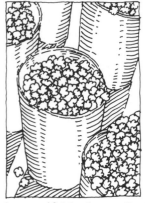

LAST WEEK I told you about how my friend Dick Caldwell puts himself to sleep at night by reading interesting data out of a Reader's Digest book called "Stories Behind Everyday Things." Dick loaned me the book after depressing me with a wagonload of details he had amassed while I ate a little wagonload of food at my favorite eatery.

Well, now I'm hooked, too. I read it when I turn in, but as I said last week, I'd prefer to read it in an outhouse, if I had one. In fact, if Reader's Digest ever puts out a rural edition, they should print it on a roll of perforated paper.

All kidding aside, I've learned lots of good stuff from the book. Most of it I don't need to know, sort of like the stuff I learned when I was studying for my doctorate.

Did you know, for instance, that 6 billion quarts of popcorn are eaten in the United States each year? That comes under the C for Corn. Judging by the Beautiful Wife's eating habits, I'd have guessed it would have been more like 9 billion quarts. And I wonder why Caldwell never mentioned the fact to me because I know he got through the C's, having drilled me on the D's.

Did you know that the first guitar was a hunting bow? Here's how it worked. Hermes stole valuable cattle from Apollo. When caught, the clever fellow escaped Apollo's wrath by fashioning a lyre from his hunting bow strung with three cow-gut strings stretched across an empty turtle shell. They don't say whether Robin Hood ever serenaded Maid Marian, strumming on his archer's bow. It would make a good story though, wouldn't it?

Did you know that knives, forks and spoons didn't exist until the Renaissance? Until then folks seized food with their bare hands and tore meat off the bones with their teeth. Some folks still do and should probably read Caldwell's book and get with it.

Did you know that the average new car from Detroit contains 25 pounds of glue?

Did you know that the average kid from my third-grade class in 1945 contained 25 pounds of library paste?

No, they didn't — I was just kidding. And I couldn't find

out anything about library paste in Caldwell's book, either. So it isn't perfect.

Did you know that a Frenchman popularized potatoes in the 18th century by posting a military guard around his field during the day, then dismissed them at night? As you might expect, the peasants sneaked in as darkness fell, stole the potatoes and ate them. Before that potatoes were thought to cause everything from tuberculosis to leprosy. Now the French fry them in deep fat and cause hardening of the arteries. (That last assertion is mine.)

Did you know that Charles Dickens couldn't sleep unless his bed was aligned on a north-south axis, that Enrico Caruso preferred to sleep surrounded by 18 pillows, that Marilyn Monroe slept wearing nothing but Chanel No. 5, and that Russian noblemen attempting to sleep had servants scratch their feet to induce relaxation? Did you know that John Milton said of sleep that "Nature requires five (hours), custom takes seven, laziness takes nine and wickedness eleven?" Did you know that most of us spend a third of our lives sleeping?

I'll accept that last one if they'll rewrite it slightly to read: "Most of us spend a third of our lives sleeping, unless of course they have a friend named Dick Caldwell who recites facts to them over lunch. Then the fraction is slightly higher."

∼

# *You Can Lead a Horticulture...*

**H**OW'S THIS for a sequence of events?

**Event No. 1:** Two years ago, I got a letter from the city clerk in my home town informing me that a neighbor had reported a dead tree on my property. The clerk told me that I had two weeks to remove the tree or the city would do it for some god-awful price. I arranged to have the tree removed, then called the city clerk and asked who made the complaint, as if I didn't know. The city clerk said that "the complainant asked not to be named."

**Event No. 2:** The next day, I went to lunch at The Little

Wagon in downtown Minneapolis and told my friends of the trials and tribulations of a property owner. Time passed.

**Event No. 3:** One year ago, my colleague Kate Parry came to work one morning and told us that she had received a letter from the Minneapolis City Engineer's office. The burden of the engineer's message was that the metal house numbers on Kate's front door were one-quarter inch too small and that she must rectify the situation or face a fine. Kate looked out on the street and saw potholes big enough to lose a stagecoach in and thought someone was ribbing her. So she called the city engineer's office. "Yes," the clerk said. "We have your name and you should change your numbers immediately." "OK, OK," said Kate. "But can I ask you a question? How do you people know that my house numbers are *one-quarter inch* too small and not one-third or one-half inch too small?" The clerk said that was simple, that there were city employees who ran around with rulers and measured.

**Event No. 4:** That noon, I lunched at The Little Wagon and told my friends of Kate's plight. They had a good laugh out of that.

**Event No. 5:** This spring, I planted the medium-sized garden alongside my house.

**Event No. 6:** In mid-June, when the Seeded Simpson was at its peak, I received a letter on official stationery from the Minneapolis City Engineer's office: "Mr. Wood: It has come to our attention that you are in violation of Minneapolis City Ordinance 718.56, 'Agrarian Use of Urban Land.' The ordinance states that you are allowed two (2) square feet of vegetable garden space for every foot of lot frontage you own. This allows you a garden of one hundred (100 square feet). Your garden is in excess of that allotment and you are therefore requested to sod in eighty-five (85) square feet within two weeks, or pay a fine . . . "

Oh, goodness gracious, thought I. This, indeed, is a brave new world, when bureaucrats can keep me from growing parsnips. And then I read on.

" . . . You may apply for a two-week extension in the event you can't find a company to install sod. After that period, if the matter has not been rectified, the city will perform the work and you will be assessed $400 . . ."

Golly, willikers, thought I. I'd better get out to a sod farm on Saturday. And then I read on.

" . . . the complainant asked not to be named."

Hmmmmm. That line sounded faintly familiar. Aha! The guys from The Little Wagon were at it as usual. So I kept my lip buttoned.

**Event No. 7:** Two weeks later, Robert T. Smith, a very

thoughtful Wagoneer whose stories occasionally appear in Grit, called my wife aside at a party and wondered if I'd sodded in the garden. "Woody's a real nice guy," said Smith, "but the fellows are worried that he's a little bit naive . . ."

**Event No. 8:** I let them worry.

~

## *Squaretable Band Flunks Screen Test*

THE BETTER THAN NOTHING DIRT BAND is the contingent in which I play the tuba. Today I'm not going to talk about how badly we *play*. I'm going to talk about how bad we *look*. This requires some backing up. About a month ago, we were approached by this corporate executive in charge of making a motivation film for his company, one of those movies that urges employees on to doing better things.

"We would like you," he said, "to provide music for our

55

movie. If you do, we'll give lots of money to your favorite charity."

Well now. Was this guy on the level, asking us to be in a movie that would be seen by thousands of his company's employees? After all, there are hundreds of unemployed professional musicians in this town who are dying for work. And they can play music. Well now.

So we asked him if he had lost his senses or if his psychiatrist ever told him that he had suicidal impulses. Not at all, said the executive. He said he had heard us play on occasion and that our music would be perfect for the sound track of his movie. He explained: "This movie is aimed at helping our employees adjust to new technologies and new ways of doing things. So the movie will feature a band which got its start playing polkas and waltzes and old-fashioned music, just like your band. When rock and roll comes in, the band loses popularity, but it refuses to adjust to the times."

Aha. So we'll be the fall guys, is that right?

"Right," said the executive. "You'll provide the music for the band when it's playing the dumb, old-fashioned music. Later, the band will catch on to the new music and they'll succeed and our employees will learn from that to deal with new technologies."

The offer was sort of insulting, but we're used to that, so we trotted off to the sound studio to cut the sound track, helped by all manner of fancy technicians and sound mixers, etc. We played stuff like our theme song "Rhapsody in Liechtenstein," which starts with a clarinet glissando from "Rhapsody in Blue" and quickly segues into "Liechtensteiner Polka." As usual, we were terrible, but the executive seemed very pleased.

So when the recording session was all over, we asked the executive when we should show up for the filming of the movie.

"Oh," said he, "We're hiring *actors* to play your roles. Your job is finished. We'll take what we can use from this recording session. And we'll plug it into movie footage in which there's a bunch of actors pretending to play polkas and waltzes on instruments they don't know how to play."

Gentle Grit readers, are you getting my drift?

If not, let me recap: The Better Than Nothing Dirt Band plays so badly that we have been tapped, from all the musicians in Minneapolis, to play music that typically would be performed by a terrible, out-of-date band. So far, so good. But now comes the cruncher: Even though they don't mind that we play badly, each and every member is so ugly, so hopelessly out of tune (as it were) with what people like to look at, that they're hiring profes-

56

sional actors to impersonate us. That's the unkindest cut, to quote another writer. To make it worse, when we left the studio, the executive asked if he could rent my tuba, a 1947 Conn model with more dents in it than in Evel Knievel's skull.

So I said, "That'll be 50 bucks, please" and the executive agreed. Maybe I could use the rent I receive for the down payment on a facelift.

~

## Squaretable Conversation Borders On The Bizarre

 The other day, I edited a piece of copy in which a reporter had used the word "literary" and the typesetter substituted it with "literate." I missed the change and the next day, in the newspaper, the story said such-and-such a publisher never "published books that were very literate." Right now they're taking bets in the newsroom on whether the reporter or the book publisher will catch me first. And which limb he/they will break when they do.

A depressing situation, but ameliorated at lunch in The Little Wagon that very day. When the talk of Middle Eastern politics got too depressing, some of the long-timers around the table got to talking about some of the baggy-pants journalists of the past, some of whom had very little gray matter upstairs and some of whom probably had too much for their own good.

Dan Byrne told of a St. Paul photographer who was sent to the Twin Cities airport to shoot a picture of the Dionne quintuplets' arrival in the Twin Cities back in 1940. "They came out of the plane one by one," recalled Dan. "And John (not his real name) took a shot of each as they came. One, two, three, four . . . After the last kid appeared on the exit ladder, John turned to the reporter and said, 'By golly, there are *five* of them!' "

Someone else told the story about an ancient night copy editor who hadn't been out of the building except to sleep for about 40 years. He edited a piece of Associated Press copy about a kidnapping in Florida in which the kidnappers asked that a rubber container of ransom money be dropped off a bridge into a river. The AP story read thusly: "When the money was dropped into the river, a man in a wetsuit emerged from beneath the surface of the river, snared the ransom package and was immediately arrested by local police."

The next morning the story appeared in the paper with one syllable missing. "A man in a suit emerged from beneath the surface of the river. . . . " When asked by his superior why he had deleted "wet," the grizzled old copy editor said this: "Why, tarnation, any fool would know if a guy was in a river his suit would be *wet*!"

Star Tribune photographer Earl Seubert remembered going out on a story with a crafty old reporter who was known for scooping the rival newspapers in town. "We had a report of a hotel fire and we got there first. It wasn't much, just a smoldering mattress in one room. There were no people in the room, just a cat beside the bed. The old reporter said to me, 'Get a shot of that cat,' so I did. Then the reporter asked the hotel manager whose cat it was. The manager said he didn't know and the reporter said, 'Gee, my grandson loves cats. Could I take it home?' The hotel manager said, sure, and off we went. As we raced back to the paper to develop the picture, the old reporter tossed the cat out of the speeding car. I was appalled, but the reporter said, 'Tomorrow morning, no other paper in town is going to have a picture of a cat in a burning hotel room.' "

The stories got wilder and wilder as luncheon progressed. Perhaps the most outrageous was the one from Robert T. Smith, a columnist who was city editor of the Minneapolis Tribune in the '50s. He told of sending a jaded old crime reporter to Plainfield, Wis., to see what was up. What was up turned out to be Ed Gein, the psychopathic grave robber who upholstered his furniture in human skin and probably supped on the flesh that skin had encased. When the reporter got to Plainfield, he called in. "What's up? asked Smith. "Smitty," replied the reporter, "I think we've got something here that *borders* on the bizarre."

~

# Linoleum, Eighth Wonder of the World

**T**HE OTHER DAY at lunch, we talked about all the wonderful inventions that have come to fruition in the past century or so. Some of the older journalists remembered the days of lead type and wondered at the slick efficiency of computer typography. Still others asked how we'd get along without automatic transmissions in our automobiles or how we could do our work without the marvels of flight through the air.

I told about living on our hobby farm and the inconvenience of not having running water in the house. "But we had an electric pump at the well on the hill. And we had electric lights. I think if I had to give up all modern inventions but one, I'd opt to keep electricity," said I sagely.

"Giving up all modern inventions, but one?" mused Steve Alnes. "Thereby, gentleman, hangs a tale."

We all sat up straight and paid attention. Steve Alnes, you see, is the closest thing to an intellectual that our luncheon group possesses and so we have to listen hard just to understand what he's talking about.

So straighten up, gentle reader, and try to understand if I understood this tale told by Alnes, signifying something.

Seems that not too many years ago, Alnes's wife, Peggy, worked for a newspaper and was sent out to interview a 100-year-old woman. The discussion turned to progress and recent advances in technology.

"Finally," continued Alnes, "Peggy asked the old woman 'What's the one modern invention that you wouldn't give up?' "

The old woman knitted her brow and thought and thought and thought, while Peggy wondered what was coming. Airplanes? Automobiles? Television? Radio? Penicillin? Open heart surgery? Finally, the old lady looked up from her rumination, with a self-satisfied look. And this is what she said:

"Linoleum."

Linoleum.

A spectrum of male chauvinist hogs to piglets who sit at our table chuckled at that one, I'll tell you.

But, Alnes said, when you think of it, when you think of this old lady who had grown to womanhood on the wintry wastes of rural northern Minnesota, probably in a log cabin with a planked floor, when you think of the scrubbing and drudgery and the infernal men coming in from the infernal milking with infernal cow manure on their infernal shoes, then you see the logic of her point of view. And you have to admire her for it.

Linoleum. Linoleum meant to that old woman what the aqueducts meant to a Roman and what the stirrup meant to Charlemagne.

Her response called to mind the linoleum on the farmhouse kitchen floor where I grew up. It was World War II, you couldn't buy new linoleum, and ours had the finish worn off, a depressing sight. I came home from school one afternoon to find that my mother had painted the old linoleum with blue enamel, which had dried. There she was on her hands and knees, dipping a small sponge into a can of yellow paint and blotting onto the blue a design of sunbursts every 12 inches. My mother would have agreed with the old lady.

~

## A Fine Epistolary Rage

**M**Y FRIEND Tom has had his battles with those dog-goned computer letters that cram everyone's mailbox these days. Tom is a witty fellow who, for instance, decided to take a computer-written dunning letter from American Express at its word. He telephoned the man whose name was typed at the bottom, while the man was entertaining at a dinner party. The man got a bit testy, so Tom just told him that the wonderful letter he'd just received said that he was supposed to get in contact IMMEDIATELY.

Those doggoned computer letters keep coming:

DEAR MR. DAVE WOOD, do your neighbors on ELLIOT AVENUE, MINNEAPOLIS, know that you, MR. DAVE WOOD, may already have won $10,000,000?

I keep friend Tom posted on the good ones and he reciprocates. Tom is a public relations man for Northwestern Bell Telephone Co. Recently he sent along a letter he'd gotten from a local public relations firm. It began DEAR PUBLIC RELATIONS SPECIALIST: It went on to say how Tom could benefit from the services of the firm and then was signed by its president — who turned out to be a longtime friend of Tom's.

Occasionally Tom and I fake computer letters and send them to each other. Here's a sample of one Tom sent me recently from a bogus outfit called DREAM STRUCTURES OF A LIFETIME:

DEAR MR. DAVE WOOD: MR. WOOD, we know that you are a famous GOURMET/NEWSPAPER REPORTER/RACONTEUR/BON VIVANT. We know, MR. WOOD, that you enjoy great EATING, COOKING, WRITING, STORY-TELLING and HIGH LIVING.

And so, MR. DAVE WOOD, you have been selected to receive, absolutely free, no strings attached, our deluxe model re-creation of St. Paul's famous BLUE HORSE RESTAURANT, in easy-to-assemble kit form, delivered to the site of your choice, and complete with fully equipped kitchen. ... We are making this offer, MR. DAVE WOOD, because we consider you to be a MAJOR OPINION LEADER, and we feel that our product on your site is the best type of advertising we could ask for. Official retail price of this kit, easily assembled in one evening, is $999,898.98, F.O.B. ... The kit will be delivered, ABSOLUTELY FREE. ... You pay ONLY the $999,898.98 purchase price, plus state and local taxes and cost of building permits. NOTHING MORE. ... That means, MR. DAVE WOOD, monthly payments of only $4,328.85. ...

Get the picture?

Last week, MR. TOM LEE, PUBLIC RELATIONS SPECIALIST, sent me a packet recently received by Northwestern Bell Telephone Company's office on Beard Avenue. The address said NRTHWSTRN BELL TELE, 4701 BEARD AVENUE S., MINNEAPOLIS. Inside, the letter said:

"This to certify that NRTHWSTRN BELL TELE is eligible for 2 big Million Dollar Prizes in American Family Publishers MULTI-MILLION DOLLAR SWEEPSTAKES. ...

But also it warned that this was MR. NRTHWSTRN BELL's last chance and that he would have to act immediately and beat it down to the post office and send in the entry order by such and such a date.

Funny, eh? But not as funny as when the late Minneapolis Star columnist Don Morrison received a computer letter from Madrid, Spain. It had Don's correct address, but the name was a bit off:

DEAR MISS DONNA MORRISON: We have carefully examined your life and your accomplishments. Our blue ribbon panel has concluded that you, MISS MORRISON, should appear in our yearbook, "Famous People of the World." Certainly you'll want to purchase a copy of this book, bound in simulated buckram, for only $47.95. . . . "

I hope MR. NRTHWSTRN BELL will beat it down to the post office, so MR. NRTHWSTRN BELL can win one of those million- dollar prizes. Then MR. BELL won't have to ask for a rate increase. That should free up some money so I can pay my taxes, so the post office can continue to send me all those junk letters that cram our mailboxes.

~

## *Coach Juggernaut Meets Match on Mat*

 **M**Y FRIENDS AT The Little Wagon come to me with tickets for Twins baseball games, Viking football games, North Star hockey games. I sort of brush them off in that well-coordinated way of mine. Then I stumble away and trip on the curb, not knowing my right foot from my left, my hat from glove, et cetera, et cetera, et cetera. Finally someone said, "Woodie, I know why you don't like athletics, why you never go to games. It's because you're so uncoordinated that it's tough to watch you get into a car." Maybe so, maybe so. But somehow I think it goes back to my junior high school days and The Coach That Everybody Feared.

Let's call him Coach Juggernaut, because that's how he was built. Tough as nails, handsome, with straight teeth and a crooked smile. On the physical education field, he always wore a referee's striped shirt and a whistle cord with which he whipped the rumps of those who lagged behind. Guess whose rump got the most welts?

I wasn't Coach Juggernaut's only target. There were kids from the country who hadn't seen a football until their arrival in town at ninth grade. Juggernaut berated them for their vast moral ignorance and expected them to get with it, assigning them to positions they had never played, then cursing them for their failures.

63

Coach Juggernaut belonged in the Big Ten, not junior high school. Come to think of it, if all were right with the world, he didn't belong in the Big Ten, either. I'd always loved school, but after a few weeks under Juggernaut's rude tutelage, I came to dread even history class, because P.E. came right afterward.

At noon, Juggernaut had charge of the gymnasium and it was a perfect opportunity for him to show students and faculty the stuff of which he and his charges were made. He did this by tossing wrestling mats on the floor and challenging kids to go at it with him. If they were silly enough to try, well, Juggernaut showed everyone their stuff by beating it out of them. Grade- and high-schoolers eating hot lunch on the gymnasium balcony were treated to this spectacle Monday through Friday. It was less appetizing than the macaroni casserole, bread and army surplus peanut butter.

Then one day — Feb. 1, 1951, I believe — at about 12:07, Coach Juggernaut threw out a challenge to a junior we'll call Knut Knutson, a big pudgy farm kid. Knut was real smart in school, but never showed much interest in sports, a cardinal sin in a small town if you weigh more than 150 pounds. "Hey, Knut," said Coach J. "You big fat slob. Are you too chicken to go out for football? Or are you too dumb?"

"No," said Knut slowly and with a grin. "Neither."

"Well, how about a little wrestling match?"

"OK," said Knut, lumbering onto the mat.

Coach Juggernaut's sadistic paws reached for the kid with the flannel shirt and the blue jeans. That kid picked Juggernaut up, held him over his head, then slammed him on to the mat and then sat on him. Whenever Juggernaut tried to get away, Knut raised his rump a bit, then sat down a little harder.

Hot lunch diners cheered, Coach Juggernaut said "I give," and Knut released him to the locker room, a shameful sight. Coach Juggernaut resigned three months later.

It was the greatest moment in my young life except for when Truman beat Dewey three years earlier. Knut went on to earn his Ph.D. I followed suit. That's the story.

(*Author's note:* Not all my ideas for stories come from so close to my natal place. Often one is forced by wife and work and whim to widen our world beyond The Little Wagon to work one's warmth and weal in far-flung wheel ruts, as the next two stories attest.)

~

# Hands Across the Water

THE GRASS IS ALWAYS greener on the other side of the fence. And that doesn't apply just to Pa's Guernseys, who could step through a three-strand fence into Mr. Berg's pasture with the grace of Mikhail Baryshnikov. I'm down here working for a week with a bunch of fine young journalism teachers. We're in a fine hotel on the Gulf of Mexico, the seafood is great, the people hospitable.

But it's hot, it's humid, and I'm working 10 hours a day. A few nights ago, as I trudged through the blistering sand after a dip in the tepid Gulf, I thought of the days when I was a teacher and had three months off and how the Beautiful Wife and I could spend a month or two every summer in England, that cool spot of green, that sceptered isle. I'm an anglophile, there's no doubt about it, and I longed for those green days, when I was one and 30, and my True Love said to me, "Hey, chubby, let's go to Great Britain in July."

So I showered and dressed thinking about the Lake Country, Oxford, and a fine little hotel we stayed at in Moreton-on-Marsh, the Cotswalds. And, of course, London, where we honeymooned. London, the greatest city in all the world. I made my way to the cocktail lounge on the top floor of the Hilton, ordered something cool and looked out at the shimmering Gulf, which was also simmering enough to cook an egg, if you had the inclination. A couple sat down next to me. I smiled and because they smiled back, I introduced myself. They returned the favor.

The man turned out to be Andrew Neville and his comely wife was Julia. And their accents were British. Hmmm, thought I.

We made small talk and I discovered Andrew was a financial consultant who lives in Manchester, in England's industrial heartland. He also serves on the city council and is a leader in the Conservative Party. He married Julia, a native of Northern Ireland, six years ago and they obviously enjoy each other immensely. Our conversation went something like this:

**Julia:** We come to Florida twice a year. We just love it here.

**Dave:** Sort of hot and humid, isn't it? I've been in England several times. What a wonderful country, so civilized. I envy you for living there.

**Andrew:** If there was a place for me in the United States, I'd move here in a shot. . . .

It turns out that Julia and Andrew have a cottage in the mountains, but they never go there much, preferring the sights and sounds of Florida. I ooh and aah over my mental picture of their cottage and they just smile and look at my tanned forearms, something they don't see much of in their homeland. Finally, Julia of the creamy British complexion, flushes and makes a confession. "Do you know that we've lived two hours from London for six years and I've never been there?"

Goodness gracious, am I losing my grip on reality? Here's this wonderful, witty woman, a woman full of a sense of adventure and she's never been in London with its magnificent parks, its friendly people, its theaters. . . .

Andrew and Julia were such a charming couple, I couldn't hold their taste against them and we've bumped into each other on a few occasions since that brief encounter a few days back. But I never failed to twit Julia about never going to London. At our last meeting, Andrew had a big grin on his face. "We just received a wire (that's the way they talk over there). Julia finally must go to London. We've been invited to dine with Prime Minister Thatcher next month. It's an invitation we can hardly refuse."

Poor Julia.

~

# Hands Across the Sky

***Dateline:*** *Sovicille, Italy*

**W**E ROCKETED DOWN the hillside from San Gimignano, heading for two-week stay at a workers' cottage on a huge Italian farm near Siena, Italy. This had been all my idea, you see, and I was just a bit edgy and defensive about it. After we picked up groceries in the little town of Poggibonsi, the Beautiful Wife expressed some concern as well: "What if our house doesn't have a refrigerator, what if all this food just *rots!*"

"Ha, ha," said I nervously. "Dry pasta and canned tomato paste does not rot, My Own Beloved. So don't worry."

But I was nervous. What if the old farm was a dump? I'd plunked my money down months ago and it wasn't refundable. This wasn't like renting a hotel for a night. We followed our written directions and turned onto a blindingly white dirt road and plunged up the hill through a chestnut forest. As the 6 kilometers between Us and It ticked off, the tension rose in our little Fiat. Finally, a sign: "Villa This Way." We turned and drove through a stone gate and looked at the villa and saw Signor Pellegrini, the owner. He smiled, we smiled. So far, so good.

We introduced ourselves and the very courtly gentleman said, "Come this way, please." We followed him through a high stone gate and then we saw it, a cottage hundreds of years old, with a tile roof and walls that must have been three feet thick. A chicken from the foreman's house scratched in the driveway.

I knew it. I just knew it. I knew this had been a good idea from the start. Inside, the B.W. found a modern kitchen, with gas stove and refrigerator, a modern bathroom, with shower, sink, stool and bidet, probably not enjoyed by hired men of centuries past. The living quarters were beautifully furnished in antiques. Signor Pellegrini left us with good wishes.

Whew! What a relief! For the next two weeks B.W. and I had the best time in memory. Behind the stone hay barn there was a big new swimming pool, where we swam morning, noon and night. On lazy days we'd read in easy chairs in the garden of the 18th-century church on the farm grounds. Every day we walked out onto the narrow roads that cut through the farm's forests and meadows, wondering how the Pellegrinis could raise wheat, and alfalfa and goats in such a dry climate. And at night we prepared wonderful food from the region, flavored it with the local pecorino cheese or dill picked along the roadside. One of my favorite mornings was spent shelling beans in the garden and watching Signor Pellegrini work a wheatfield with his Peoria, Ill., Caterpillar and plow with two huge bottoms that turned over the orange soil in huge clumps. You can take the boy out of Wisconsin, but you can't take Wisconsin out of the boy, I guess.

In the evenings, we sat out and looked into the black sky and saw the Big Dipper and thought of the astronomer Ptolemy, whose descendents lived on this farm for 1,000 years. And most important, we befriended the Pellegrinis, Aurelio and his wife, Cati. They invited us to lunch, we had them to dinner. We talked about farm prices and how difficult it is for farmers, both in the U.S. and in Italy. We talked of food and customs and literature. Signora Pellegrini liked Shakespearean comedies, my wife liked the Italian novelist Italo Calvino, who was dying in nearby Siena as we spoke. Signor Pellegrini and I liked John Steinbeck.

Fourteen days came and went and we had to say our *arrivedercis,* sadly. I wanted to embrace Signor Pellegrini in the Italian manner, but you can't take Wisconsin out of the boy, so I shook his hand. As we headed for Rome, B.W. said, "Signor Pellegrini looked as if he wanted to embrace you."

I know we'll be back there as soon as time and money permit. Until then, we'll remember the green-black chestnut forests, the walks on the little roads, the tinkling of goat bells, the limpid blue sky, the orange soil and our new-found friendship with the Pellegrini family.

(*Author's note:* In 1987, the B.W. and I returned to Pellegrinis farm at their kind invitation to lunch. We met outside the great house, and Signor Pellegrini and I embraced. Talk about sophisticated!)

~

# Chapter 4

# Grit Readers To The Rescue

*B*easts *may convey, and tuneful birds may sing,*
*Their mutual feelings, in the opening Spring;*
*But man alone has skill and power to send*
*The heart's warm dictates to the distant friend.*

—*George Crabbe*

AS I MENTIONED in the introduction, Grit readers began writing letters to this distant friend as soon as my first column appeared. So many a time upon a midnight dreary, when I pondered weak and weary about what I can do for the morning's Grit deadline, I have turned to my file of letters from readers who hail from large and small towns across the country. In short, I let them do my work for me.

In an age when most letters to newspapers are filled with vitriol, Grit readers are an anachronism. Normally most letter writers call for the columnist's immediate dismissal. But Grit writers send missives of useful advice and encouragement and even goods of material value.

Last year, I wrote a column in which I explained how my child bride and I had been shopping in a youthful record store in Minneapolis and I had discovered two polka tapes, one by Whoopee John and one by the Six Fat Dutchmen. Ruth said, "I won't go through the checkout counter with you if you plan to buy them." I planned to buy them so she left the store first, and waited for me on the street.

Soon after the column appeared, Mr. Clarence Hinsverk, an octogenarian from Williston, N.D., wrote and asked my home address, so he could "send me something." To date I have received 20 long-play polka tapes that Clarence has re-recorded for me. That's my kind of reader. And he isn't the only reader who has brightened my life, as the columns that follow will attest.

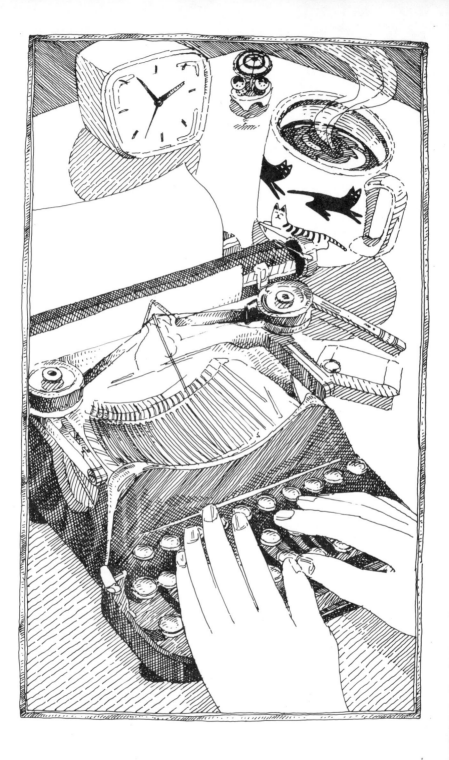

# "Some Damned Fool Wrote Me A Letter and Signed Your Name"

I READ IN THE PAPER a few weeks back that Stephen Young, the former senator from Ohio passed on. He had lived a long, productive life. Still, I was saddened to read that a man of his wit and gumption had passed from the scene.

Remember Senator Young? He's the fellow who, back in the '60s, didn't mince words when he got a hostile letter from a constituent. His standard reply to such a letter was as follows:

"Dear Mr. Smith:

"Some damned fool in my constituency wrote me a letter dated August 10 and he signed your name. I thought you would want to know.

"Sincerely,

"Senator Stephen Young."

Now that's my kind of letter writer.

I get letters like that in my daily job at the Star Tribune. Most of them are, to put it tepidly, hot. Very hot. One fellow was so incensed at the way I was running the page I'm responsible for that he wrote me a three-page, single-spaced letter without one capital letter. Understand, he knew the rules of punctuation and grammar and everything else was just as it should be. But I figure he was so peeved that he didn't want to take the time to push the shift button on his typewriter.

Grit readers aren't like that, which is one of the reasons I so enjoy writing this column. Even if the reader has an axe to grind, he or she does it in an even-handed way. I've had lots of letters lately, most of them simply chatty. But I got one the other day from Fred L. Reed of Massachusetts. He pointed out my mistake in attributing the quote, "Simplify, simplify," to Ralph Waldo Emerson, that the quote really came from Emerson's buddy, Henry David Thoreau. Of course, he was right. (Thoreau's the fellow, who, when invited to dine at Emerson's sumptuous table, only ate out of the serving platter next to him at the table. That's what I call simplifying.)

Anyway, Mr. Reed was kind, nay jocular, about the mistake. And he capitalized all the right words. As a fellow writer, he signed off with a charming wish: "Strength to your typewriter."

Mary M. Sponseller of Virginia recently wrote to comment on my column about my fatal year in the church choir and to add that I'm not the only off-key singer in this earthly choir. (When she was in fourth grade, Mary got bumped from the choir

71

of angels in a school pageant.) That made me feel great and I sang all the way to my evening and through it, too.

I don't get many letters from college professors, but recently one came from San Jose State University, penned by journalism professor Joe B. Swam. I shuddered, but what to my wondering eyes should appear but the following: "Too many columnists are dishing up raw liver these days when this old Texas country boy is looking for cornbread and pinto beans." I've never written about pinto beans and cornbread, Joe, but have you tried side pork drippings on pancakes? Methinks Joe and I are on the same wavelength.

Finally, I got a fat package the other day from Mary Stabnau of Pennsylvania. She invited me to drop by for coffee whenever I was in the neighborhood and complimented me on the outhouse story I did months back. And out of her letter dropped a whole stack of neatly pressed peach wrappers. She asked me to take them with her compliments and added, "No offense intended."

No offense taken, Mary, no offense taken.

~

# Call Me Ishmael But Don't Call Me Late for Dinner

*What's in a name? That which we call a rose*
*By any other name would smell as sweet.*

*—William Shakespeare,*
*Romeo and Juliet, II, li*

YEAH, BILL, but a name by any other name wouldn't be as funny. At least that's what my friend Mike Smith believes. Mike is an editor at the Star Tribune and when a particularly good name in the news comes across his desk, he saves it. If a friend finds such a name, it is passed on to Mike and Mike saves that, too, and so he has hundreds of names stacked up.

Mike doesn't know what he's going to do with all these names, but I know what I'm going to do with a few. Right now.

We'll start with a few chosen because they have sort of a nice ring to them.

How about *Guts Ishimatsu,* a former WBC lightweight champion?

Or *Sir Dingle Foot,* who died in 1978 after serving as Great Britain's Solicitor General?

Or *Barefoot Sanders,* a U.S. district judge? Or *Dr. Penny Wise Budoff,* a gynecologist-author who once appeared on the Phil Donahue Show?

Reading or saying aloud these wonderful names that sort of trip off the tongue, then stick in your consciousness for days and sometimes weeks, one gets a partial answer to why my friend Mike Smith collects them. *Mike Smith.* How'd you like to be stuck with a two-syllable moniker like that? That's why guys named Mike Smith and *Dave Wood* live vicariously by reveling in tongue-twisters whenever we find them.

Our tickers skipped a beat when on July 18, 1979, Mike ferreted out *Cantwell F. Muckenfuss III. Cantwell F. Muckenfuss III,* now there's a name with a ring to it. And he also fits into our next category, once you find out what he does for a living. Our next category is Names Appropriate to the Bearer's Occupation. *Cantwell F. Muckenfuss III* just happened to be senior deputy controller of the currency when Mike found his name.

Here's more in the "Appropriate" category:

Folks living around McConnell Air Force Base can sleep better nights once they know there's a public information officer in place named *Capt. Alan Defend.*

The more rabid hockey fans in the Windy City must love a Chicago Blackhawks defenseman named *Ted Bulley.*

How'd you like to be guilty of a heinous crime and come up before a magistrate named *Judge Dyer Justice Taylor?*

Given the tone these days in Washington, D.C., I'll bet the deputy director of management and the budget is up for a promotion. His name is *Bowman Cutter.*

Out at the University of Nebraska back in 1978, three of the young men on the golf team were named *Larry Sock, Randy Sock* and *Vic Carder.*

Even up here in Minnesota we have names other than Olsen and Johnson. Fellow named *Sam Solon* is a state legislator from Duluth. And there's a scholar at our College of St. Benedict who does research on violence among married couples. His name? *James Makepeace,* what else?

Some appropriate names must be embarrassing to carry around. If you were a controller of currency, would you like to be called Cantwell F. Muckenfuss III? There's that name again, which leads us to category III, Names Inappropriate to the Bearer's Occupation.

I'll give you four and then get out while the getting's good.

A gentleman from Korea who helped select the present pope is named **Cardinal Sin.** And there's the Archbishop of Manila, whose name is **Jaime Cardinal Sin.**

**David Dull** at one time edited a publication called "Editor's Guide to the United Nations." You don't see big stacks of his tome in many bookstores.

Finally, there's the director of weights and measures for the Navajo Nation — **Melvin Big Thumb.** He sounds a lot like my grandma's butcher.

(**Author's note:** Ofttimes, a column like the preceding one sparks another, as in the case of all the funny names I received from Grit readers, or part of another, as in the case of the column that follows.)

# The Morning Mail

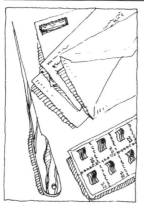

**W**ITH GASOLINE so expensive and with motel and restaurant prices shooting up, it's difficult for a working stiff like me to travel much these days. Recently, the Beautiful Wife and I spent a week in Mexico and spent more money than my father made in a year just after World War II. B.W. and I weren't exactly living high off the enchilada, either.

But I like to look on the brighter side of things. I like to think I'm lucky to be writing for a national weekly like Grit. The pay is good and I get a bonus almost every week when someone from a faraway place writes to me about last week's column. That way I get around to places I've never been for the price of a mere postage stamp. Back when I wrote for my hometown weekly, I got letters of course, but usually I never wrote back. Usually, I just hollered out the kitchen window and told the writer that he could be sued for such libelous accusations. The Whitehall Times had a limited circulation area.

But not Grit. I get letters from all over the country. One of the first came along about Christmas time from Roger Hanson of Dixon, Ill. It began, "Dear Dave: I wondered what became of you. . . . " You see, Roger Hanson was a boyhood chum and I hadn't seen him for years. Lucky for me he wrote because I thought he'd fallen off the edge of the world, and so, I was planning to write a little piece on what a mean kid he was. Now I don't dare, but at least Roger and I have started up a correspondence.

I've also added to my repertoire of bacon-grease recipes because letters of culinary delights came after I wrote about my affection for bacon-grease and Karo syrup.

Jo Kendall, who signed off as "A Greasy Grandma," tried to comfort me: "Don't worry about the flurry you may be causing among the nutritionists and M.D.s of this world. I've noted that for all the many things they write, as a whole they are not too healthy either. And I don't mean physically."

Then a letter came from Ervin J. Florin, Waterloo, Ill., who announced right off that he was a retired clergyman. My hands trembled as I read deeper into his letter because I figured he knew I had skipped church the week before. But no, he just wanted to say he grew up 30 miles from my home and that while in high school he'd debated at my alma mater. Judging from the letter, his team probably won.

More recently, my friend Mike Smith and I were bombarded with letters after I wrote about Mike's penchant for collecting humorous names. C.W. Vandenbergh of Brattleboro, Vt., told Mike that he was writing a book on church life and wondered if he had any clergymen's names to add to it. I do. When I was a student in Bowling Green, Ohio, our Lutheran minister had a lovely one: Pastor Loyal Bishop, as did the campus religious advisor, the Rev. Will Power.

Mrs. Glennis E. Hughes of Hampton, Va., also wrote Mike, as did Donald Willison of Howard City, Mich., as did genealogist Hilda Chance of Aston, Pa., who contributed one of my favorites: a New England man named Preserved Fish.

Just the other day I got a four-page letter from one Maggie Brown of Danville, Va. Maggie is 88 and legally blind, but she had to get up in the darkness at 3 a.m. to dash off an account of how she delivered Grit at the turn of the century, how her six children did the same, how her 17 foster children did so too. "Now," she concluded, "I can't get to sleep."

So you see there's a travel bonus for this nosy journalist in every column he writes. It's so much fun I could almost do it for nothing. But don't tell my publisher — or the B. W. Just keep the letters coming.

～

## Illinois Postmaster
## Nails My Scalp to Usage Mast

**G**RIT READER Paul E. Lockwood is the postmaster in Hoyleton, Ill., and he recently took issue with me on my column about junk mail and computer letters.

"This is to inform you," wrote Lockwood, "that the Post Office does not send junk letters. All we do is deliver them."

Good point, Mr. Lockwood. It was a careless mistake of language, but your note prompted me to get out of public affairs analysis and onto the top of my head, an area I know something about.

The top of my noggin is shiny, has been since I was in my mid-20s, just as my father's was before me. And my great grandad's, too. My grandpa died in his mid-80s topped with a thatch of black hair, with just a touch of gray at the temples. But he was one of those exceptions that prove the rule.

Had I been blessed with a thatch like Grandpa's, who knows? I might have succeeded as a Midwestern heartthrob. Or I could have been one of those filthy rich rock 'n' rollers with hair down to my back pockets, whacking away at a $5,000 guitar. Or even a modern-day Rasputin, spitting on the marble floors of the White House.

But oh, no, I had to fall in line with generations of genetic skinheads who provide so many gag lines for hirsute types who make barbers rich. And for the barbers. Recently I did a story about Moler Barber College. I jumped into the chair for a $2 trim and said jokingly that with my angelic wisps, I should get a discount. Student barber Gail Connet quipped back: "With you, I should charge extra for a finder's fee."

That's the way it goes if you're a baldy. Baldy, that's a name my shiny-pated father won't put up with. He'd rather be called Forecloser on Widows and Orphans than Baldy. If you're bald, you try for the rejoinder, but you give up quickly enough. One guy razzed my father about his lack of hair. Pa shot back with "You can't have hair and brains both." The wise guy lay in wait: "Huh! We all know that grass doesn't grow in concrete."

And so it goes for baldies, who when wandering through

Arizona, the top of our heads peels in the blistering sun, or when trudging through the rain forests of Washington state, water streams down onto our bifocals. (Bald people always wear glasses.) We're ambulatory advertisements for the conservationists who want to reforest our hillsides to prevent erosion.

But let the hairy apes laugh. My Beautiful Wife says she thinks bald guys are sexy. When she says that, I posture in front of the mirror like Yul Brynner, then settle for a limpid imitation of Kojak. Good enough. It's sweet of B.W. to say my shiny dome is sexy. But when you stop to think about it, being an H.W. (Hairless Wonder) has its practical advantages:

1. I don't spend half a fortune on pomades and lotions to keep an unruly mop from making me look like Uriah Heep.

2. We never need call the Roto-Rooter man to grind away through a bushel of my hair just so we can drain our bathtub.

3. I never make $25 trips to a stylist called Pierre of Minnesota to get my follicles massaged and my locks twisted into the latest fashion.

4. I save money on combs and blow dryers and all that stuff. When I get up in the morning I comb my hair with a damp washcloth.

5. When I cook for guests, there's not a strand of embarrassing hair in the consomme.

6. When B.W. goes for popcorn at the Orpheum, she has no trouble finding my shiny dome in the darkness among the shaggy types who surround me.

So I say: Hail To Baldness! Long May It Wave! No, that's not right. . . .

~

# Gary Bailey, Rte. 4, Menomonie, Wis.

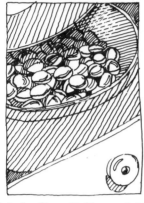

**B**ACK IN MARCH I wrote about Larkin Valley School community club and all the fun we had before the folks in that valley discovered PTA. Soon after, I received a letter from Grit reader Gary Bailey, who farms outside Menomonie, Wis. He said when he attended Ideal School, he and his friends didn't eat sandwiches and Jell-O during the normal course of a day's event. They ate goiter pills, as many as they could sneak out of the big round box kept in Miss Scovel's desk. Gary Bailey and his friends at Ideal had nothing on us 80 miles away.

For Grit readers who didn't grow up in Wisconsin, that might require some explanation. In the prehistoric days before iodized salt was commonly available, Wisconsin kids walked around sprouting big goiters, so the state department of education introduced a program in which we each got a goiter pill once a week from Gary Bailey's Miss Scovel and my Miss Hanson and the other fine women who struggled with our illiteracies for 30 dollars a month.

Now goiter pills weren't as bad as they sound. They didn't taste like iodine. The state department of education saw to that. Instead, they tasted like chocolate. Sort of like a miniature Horlick's Malted Milk Tablet, if you remember those.

So when Miss Hanson got out the purple box on Friday, it was some event. She'd pass out one pill to a customer, we'd pop them and sit real quiet, savoring the sweet chocolaty juices that began to flow. Better than Ma's pumpkin pie, better even than a chew off a Bit O' Honey. Because they were free. And then Miss Hanson would put the purple box high up in the old wooden supply cabinet, near the stack of Dick and Jane books that awaited an increase in first grade from two students to three or maybe even four.

Soon the last lingering flavor of chocolate had left our scruffy little palates and temptation set in. We'd look longingly at the cabinet and the treasure held within it. Maybe if Miss Hanson left the room, we could dart over there, grab a handful of iodized chocolate pellets and be in business for a week. Maybe we could and maybe we did, but I'm not going to risk Miss Hanson's wrath by admitting it. Leave that to Gary Bailey of Ideal School, near Menomonie.

And goiter pills weren't all we ate at Larkin Valley School. Some kids ate color crayons, not the Crayola variety, but the waxy ones that got limp as summer approached. The black ones tasted a lot like the licorice that Pa used to bring home from Stumpf's store. And we nibbled on soap erasers, too. My chi-chi city friends scoff when I tell them that. And I scoff at them when they tell about the wonderful meal of tofu they ate the night before. Far as I can tell soap erasers are about the same as tofu when it comes to taste, texture and the rubbery feeling you have when you're finished.

Some of the kids at Larkin Valley who suffered from God-knows - what vitamin deficiency always waited for art class, when Miss Hanson brought out the gallon jar of library paste. M-m-m-m good! When Miss Hanson had her back turned, Jimmy Breska would swoop a grubby index finger into the big jar, slide it through expertly, pull out a big glob and pop it into his gaping maw, roll it around like a cow chewing her cud, then swallow and settle back on his desk in a satisfied stupor. Come to think of it I did the same thing and I could go for a blob right now. Maybe it would be even better spiked with a *soupcon* of Tabasco sauce.

Bon Appetit!

~

## Bailey Redux

I HADN'T HEARD from Gary Bailey for half a year and although I didn't think about him every waking minute, I wondered what had happened to him. Today, I got a letter and it was like hearing from a long-lost brother.

He wrote to second my motion that Nut Goodies and Salted Nut Rolls were really great candy bars. Speaking of nuts, Gary must be something of a nut when it comes to writing letters, because he even wrote the Pearson Co. and told them he thought their products were great. And get this: The Pearson Candy Co., which is in St. Paul, not as I had said in Minneapolis, must also be a bit nutty because they wrote back!

Those are the kind of nuts we need more of.

Anyway, Gary went from candy bars to where you eat them, the movies.

"You are right!!" wrote Gary. "Gene Autry was the King of the Cowboys. To this day, if the Angels (owned by old Gene) make the playoffs, I start pulling for them." He said Hopalong Cassidy was second on his list. "Don't get me wrong, I liked Roy Rogers. I guess I liked a lot of them, including 'Lash' Larue and

Wild Bill Elliot. It seems we see eye to eye on a good many things."

But not on everything, Gary. I always thought "Lash" La-Rue was a real jerk.

Then Gary remembered for me the old Grand Theatre in Menomonie, his favorite childhood hangout: "Kids like me could never understand why the grownups would want to go to the other theater in town, the Orpheum, and see Esther Williams or Betty Grable in a Technicolor musical when they could go to 'The Bloody Bucket,' which was the nickname of Grand, because it specialized in westerns, Bugs Bunny shorts and serials like The Phantom."

Gary bemoaned the demise of the Grand in 1950: "Progress arrived on the scene and it was leveled and gave way to, of all things, a parking lot! I had lost an old and dear friend."

Gary Bailey is my kind of guy. The old Pix still stands in Whitehall. Unfortunately it's now a defunct country-and-western saloon. But I think the old projection booth is still there. If I ever find out where Rte. 4, Menomonie, is, I'm going to go pick up Gary Bailey, slip a rented "Springtime in the Rockies" onto the projector spool and watch in the dark silence Gene and Frog Millhouse do their stuff. What say, Gary?

~

# Guyneth Walker: Hog Butcher to Atwood

GUYNETH WALKER is 66, lives on a farm near Atwood, Ill. Some book publisher with a modicum of intelligence — if there still are such ducks — would do well to get in touch with her. Understand that Guyneth isn't hot to sell anything. But she did write a manuscript for her granddaughter, 10-year-old Becky Walker of Zion, Ill.

Guyneth sent a copy to me in Minneapolis with a note that said she thought my column was OK. Anyone like that deserves some attention, so I read on. Guyneth said that all her grandchildren adore stories. Granddaughter Becky liked stories of the long ago. And Becky also liked to read letters. So her grandmother sat down and wrote about the long ago in a series of fictional letters from a young girl named Kathryn to her cousin Viola. The year is 1928. Kathryn lives in White Heath, Ill., Viola in DeWitt, Mich.. In these carefully crafted epistles, Kathryn tells about life on the farm, about New Year's Day celebrations, about school, Valentine's Day and its fancy fold-up honeycomb hearts. Remember? And about church and what the menfolk did in the fields.

And she writes from Prairie Dell School about butchering day: "Dear Viola: I awoke at 5 o'clock this morning. A fire was blazing in the woodlot and water was heating in the big iron butchering kettles. . . five men who came to help. . . were standing out there by the fire. Uncle Jake shoots the hogs. Mr. Anderson and Daddy swish each dead hog around in a barrel of boiling water. Then they swing it onto the butchering table and scrap (sic) off its hair. Several men hook the skinned hog up to a parallel bar, cut it open and clean it out. They cut it into halves, then put it on the butchering table to cut into pieces.

"Grandma came to help with the cooking. . . . The men would have tenderloin and liver, cut up in time for Mamma to cook it for dinner. She plans to make gravy, mash potatoes, bake biscuits, put sauerkraut, pickles, jelly and cottage cheese on the table, and serve butterscotch pie and apple pie for dessert. I want to get home (from school) before Grandma leaves. She always fries little pats of sausage and everyone tastes and decides if it needs more salt.

"Mamma doesn't like butchering day. The smell of fresh meat makes her sick. The men track in mud and snow. . . . Daddy had six hogs butchered today. Grandpa and Grandma get all the meat from one hog. The neighbors who helped will each get a package of sausage and spareribs.

"Aunt Alice said she would help with the meat Saturday. She will make our sausage cakes for Mamma to fry down and can. She will help Daddy rub sugar-cure into the hams, shoulders and bacons. They wrap those in clean flour sacks and brown paper and hang them from the rafters in the oats bin in the barn. We eat them in springtime and early summer and they are delicious."

But no more delicious than Guyneth's epistolary trip into the past. After reading her manuscript, I got crazy to call her. With some help from information, I gave her a jingle. Guyneth has a soft, sweet voice and chuckled a bit when she found out who was calling. She said that "the names are fictitious. I'm really Kathryn." And Viola? "A cousin in Michigan." Her name?

"Ah, Wayne Valentine. He was the only cousin I had up there."

Had she tried to publish the manuscript? "Yes, but the editor said it lacked a plot." Where were those dummies publishing? "Minneapolis." Sorry about that. Will she keep writing? "If my grandchildren want me to."

Sharpen your pencil, Guyneth, and let Minneapolis dummies miss out on what Granddaughter Becky won't.

~

# Dells Defender
# Decimates Detractor

A FEW WEEKS AGO, I received a marvelous letter from Grit reader Janice Koehler of Wisconsin Dells, Wis. Not only was her letter marvelous, it also gently reminded me that columnists have a tremendous responsibility to be fair, that one reason some of us have fallen into disrepute is that some of us are very susceptible to taking a cheap shot once in a while and hurting people out there in Readerland, folks we don't even know.

Understand that most of us certainly don't mean to hurt people and usually do so in the heat of composition or in the near nervous breakdowns caused by tomorrow's deadline or in the occupational hazard of being hard-hitting, tough and to the point. One reason I love writing for Grit is that it's an upbeat publication devoted to the good news that still breaks among us, whereas daily newspapers over the years have developed a formula that says good news is no news and bad news sells papers.

For more than a century Grit has demonstrated that the bad news formula isn't the only formula around. And for that I'm grateful.

Janice Koehler's letter hit home because just before I received it, I was drinking coffee with a colleague up here in Minneapolis and we were talking about how local newspapers have more than their share of enemies in any town and as writers for these papers we're often the target of tirades that wouldn't happen in any other business.

Turns out my friend is attending a French class at the University of Minnesota.

Let him tell the story: "After the first couple of classes people learned that I work at the newspaper. When class ended, other students would come up to me and say, 'Boy, I can't stand the paper you work for. Used to subscribe. But I canceled. I just can't believe how terrible that paper is.' "

My friend said that sort of hurt, because he works hard for our paper and thinks it's a good newspaper trying to be better. "But when you work for a newspaper, you get that sort of stuff," he said. "If I'd worked at a delicatessen, my fellow students wouldn't come up and say, 'Hey, do I ever hate your deli. You've got the worst bagels in town.' "

Anyway, Janice Koehler wrote to express her disappointment that I called Wisconsin Dells a "tourist trap" when I wrote of a delightful outing the Beautiful Wife and I had on a recent wedding anniversary. Janice said that she and her late husband had moved to the Dells 17 years ago. "When he died three years ago, people wondered if I would move back to Chicago. No way. I love this little town.

"Sure, if you want to take in everything the Dells has to offer, you can, indeed, spend a small fortune! But please, give the Dells a chance. . . . I work in a drug store in town, and believe me, when Labor Day comes, all of us Dells workers are pretty tired, but most of us hate to see the season come to an end. . . . We really and truly enjoy the visitors, not just their money. We try to be helpful by making suggestions as to how they can see the most for the least.

"Thanks for reading this far, and for allowing me to get this off my chest, and coming to the defense of a town I have sunk roots into, and will hold fast, God willing."

And thank you, Janice Koehler, for reminding me to stop being a smarty-pants at the expense of honest, decent people such as you, people who work hard for a living and are closer to the flesh and blood of the matter than a columnist who drives past once in a blue moon.

~

# My Life as a Literary Critic

**I** **TAUGHT WRITING** for 20 years before I became a writer. As a teacher I saw some good writing, but never enough and that was discouraging. I eventually left the classroom. Nowadays, I see all kinds of good writing, some of it from my former students.

Lots of the good writing that I see doesn't get seen by many other people. But I get to see some because readers send me their efforts to ask what I think. Recently, Grit reader LaVale Mills of Hamilton, Ala., sent me a letter about her love of writing and an example of it. As most amateur writers do, her cover letter was full of apologies and doubts.

"I have always enjoyed writing. I am enclosing something I wrote just this week. My problem is, I use colloquialisms and also I come from a very unique family. We have several expressions that only other members of our clan understand. These also find their way into what I write. . . . what I write is just me! If you have time would you please read it and give me an opinion?"

OK, LaVale, you asked for it.

So you use colloquialisms? Tsk-Tsk! Heck, LaVale, you're in good company. I think "Huckleberry Finn" is the greatest American novel written in the 19th century. And it's loaded with colloquial language. That's Twain's genius and yours too — writing the way people talk.

And that family of yours! Using expressions only understood within the clan. My, my! I don't know if it's any consolation, or if we're good company, but so does my family. And, as a writer, I try to use them whenever I can. When I use them rather than textbook language, the words sort of jump off the page. Yours do, too, LaVale.

LaVale, when my pa gets a taste of coffee that burns his lips, he always says "Humph. Must have been cooked on green grubs." What does that mean, Pa? It means if you ever manage to get a green stump lit, it makes a real hot fire. Oh. That makes sense.

In our family, when we're sick, we eat buttered toast with hot milk poured over it. My grandma always called that "Graveyard Stew." Isn't that great? I think it's a better line than any I read in Hawthorne's "The Scarlet Letter."

When a member of our family has diarrhea, we refer to that unpleasant malady as "The Green Apple Quick-step." Somehow that makes things easier.

The story LaVale sent me had to do with why she liked rainy days and I knew I'd found a winner. It's easy to write about liking sunny days — and boring to read. "I've never heard a raindrop fall that wasn't music to my ears," writes LaVale. "I think it is lovely and graceful as it falls. It seems to me the mud puddles it produces are works of art and a rainbow is one of the most beautiful productions of God's artistic handiwork. . . . It was in 1973 and guess who was almost 10 months pregnant. That's right — good ol' rain-lover me. The rain was falling in a 'flat piece' as Paw Hughes used to say and I was still enjoying it. The flood lasted several days . . .

"My Grandpaw Kennedy loved rain as much as Paw Hughes. I've heard an Uncle tell about . . . when it rained so much the cotton rotted in the fields. He said one day he saw Grandpaw Kennedy walking around his lost crop, whistling. Uncle said, 'The crops are gone!' To which Grandpa replied, 'Yes, but we sure had some pretty rain.' "

LaVale Mills, you've got nothing to worry about. Keep on writing. I confer my admiration for your composition in a "flat piece."

~

## Mrs. Reich liked Gavin Better

**L**AST WEEK, I wrote about my first day at Larkin Valley School, back in 1942. Boy-oh-boy, am I ever glad that's over! I don't mean the column. I mean the school. I just never had the knack for it.

A few weeks back, I had the occasion to visit a grade-school buddy by the name of Gavin Strand. I've written about him before. He was the guy that my favorite teacher, Mrs. Lily Reich, liked better than me. You know the kind of guy. Gavin was the kind of guy who didn't eat chocolate-flavored goiter pills when Mrs. Reich was out of the room. Anyway, he's a college administrator now, and I'm just a hack.

It figures.

Anyway I hadn't had a long chat with Gavin for about 35 years and so when I stayed overnight at his house in Fountain City, Wis., we really chewed. Pity his poor wife, Connie, who had to sit there and listen. And what did we talk about? We talked about all the silly things we did back at Whitehall Grade School. Like the time Mrs. Reich asked us to write short stories about Thanksgiving and I handed one in about these two kids in

Holland who worked hard to buy their mother a turkey for Thanksgiving.

Apparently I wasn't the only kid in the world who didn't have a knack for lower education. Grit reader Clare Hauber of St. Marys, Penn., wrote to tell me about some howlers picked up in a 50-year teaching career. Clare, wrote, "If you cannot use them, will you please return them?" I can use them, Clare. I can use them. Try this student's malapropism on for size:

"We take our firemen for granite."

Then there was the formal dance, where "All the men wore tusks."

And the wet floor: "He almost fell on account of the humility in the floor."

And the flight that ended up in Cuba: "And then the plane got hitch-hiked."

And two cute ones about nuns:

"Sisters are not\rich because they do not need money because they have God." (What's so dumb about that, Clare?)

"A Sister never has to plan her day because God has it planned for her."

Clare also sent me some zany student definitions.

Countenance: "Someone who counts money."

Epistle: "Wife of an Apostle."

Adultery: "The sin of saying you're older than you really are."

Trigonometry: "Is when a lady marries three men at the same time."

Faith: "Knowing something even when you don't know it."

M.D.: "These letters signify mentally deficient."

Here's a student who couldn't spell monogamy:"Staying married to one woman is what is known as monotony."

I'm looking forward to this weekend with the Wife who is Beautiful. I'm going to put on my tusks, sit on the deck and drink Kool-Aid all day Saturday. We've practiced monotony as Epistle and Apostle now for 15 years. We've never taken the other for granite and we've never cared much for trigonometry. I've been countenancing my money very carefully so that next month we can take a vacation to Italy. If I don't slip on the humility of the airport concourse and our plane doesn't get hitch-hiked, we'll be in Rome by mid-September. I don't know it but I know that we'll have a great time unless You Know Who eats squid and has to phone someone who is mentally deficient.

~

# Grit Readers Sock It to Me

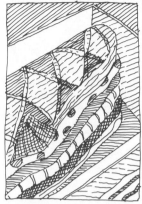

**T**ODAY, I WANT to talk about the problem that has bedeviled the marriage of my Beautiful Wife and me for the past sixth of a century.

Hold on now! I'm not announcing an imminent split with B.W. that will make the front page of the National Enquirer ("Dissipated Grit Columnist Holes up in St. Paul after Tumultuous Divorce, Ponders Becoming Jet-Setter"). Nor am I asking for sound psychological advice from a marriage counselor with several degrees in psychology and psychiatry.

Not on your life. Our problem isn't the sort that garners headlines or the $100-per-hour double-pillowed couch. B.W. doesn't run off periodically to Monte Carlo and gamble away our little cottage at the baccarat table, while I slave at the typewriter to bring home the side meat. And yours truly isn't seen with blonde Minneapolis starlets at famous downtown watering holes every weekday night, while B.W. takes in washing and mending from more fortunate and well-adjusted neighbors.

As you must have gathered by now, B.W. and I are a very well-adjusted couple, who love each other through thick and thin, sickness and health, etc., etc. Still, nothing can be perfect, right?

Right! I've just answered all you Grit readers out there, so you won't have to spend valuable money on postage. (B.W. and I are both very close with a dollar, just one other characteristic that helps make our marriage run in such an incredibly smooth manner.)

But nothing's perfect and our marriage is no exception. What's our big problem? Let me assure you it's not the crumbs I leave on the kitchen counter after making my breakfast toast and peanut butter. And it's certainly not the soggy towels I drop by the shower at night or the Christmas tree needles I scrape off when forcing the old tree through the living room door out onto the porch. No way! I'm sorry to report that the fault is all B.W.'s. Oh, sure, she never forgets my Auntie Myrtle's birthday and is always happy to have an unannounced third for dinner when an old college chum drops by Minneapolis for an evening.

But socks? Socks are B.W.'s problem. My socks.

As I write this communique, there are, reposing on my closet shelf, three boxes of single socks, washed and neatly stacked in layers, the accumulation of close to a fifth of a century of wedded bliss. Last week, as I watched a Sunday afternoon movie, I dragged them all down and tried without success to find just one of the 150 matchless anklets, and I thought back on the Single Sock of Contention that has nagged our marriage for all these years. At first, B.W.'s excuse was the laundromat. "You get in a hurry at one of those grimy places," she said, "and you leave something behind." So I bought us a house and a new washer and dryer. Still, the mates disappeared until we've made it to three shoeboxes. Where in the Goddess of Stocking's name do they disappear? "Oh, you're always traveling to Duluth or somewhere to make a speech," said B.W. "And you leave them under beds in far-flung hotels."

(Don't tell her this, but I could have gone around the world 20 times, left a sock in each hotel and still wouldn't have ended up with *three* shoeboxes full.) I mentioned this problem yesterday to colleague Robert T. Smith, who knows the marriage game better than I.

"Don't," said R.T., "try to solve this problem. Try instead to cut your losses."

And how might I do that?

"Go out," said R.T., "And buy all black socks in the same style."

(*Author's note:* I'll probably be skewered in the national press for accepting payola, but what follows recounts what happened after the preceding column about socks appeared.)

～

# No Black Sox Scandal
# For This Columnist

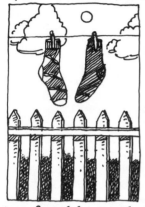

**W**ITH MOST newspapers, readers have a tendency to enjoy kicking columnists in the ribs when they're down for the count. Not so Grit readers. When a Grit columnist has a problem, Grit readers put their shoulders to your wheel and try to help extricate you from the slough you've gotten yourself into.

Several weeks ago, I wrote about the mess I'd gotten myself into with a drawer full of unmatched socks. Letters of condolence and advice flooded in from all over the country. One of the first came from Paul Morin of Williamsport, home of Grit and one of the most wonderful towns in Pennsylvania, a place from which I receive a check every week, a check I use to buy complete pairs of socks.

Paul wrote: "This is not a unique problem but one of major consequence to men. We accumulated a quantity of about 25 or 30 odd socks which absolutely could not be matched up in any combination. The cure called for drastic action. The first thing to do was to throw away all of the unmatched socks and start anew. The second thing was to make sure that socks never went into the laundry hamper. So now and for many years I have been washing my own socks by hand every morning as part of my daily bathroom chores. So far, I've never lost a sock and the sock-eating monster has been banished from our household where peace now reigns undisturbed."

Thanks for your untenable solution, Paul. It might work for some folks, but not me. I'm *lazy*. Be advised that I destroyed your letter before the Beautiful Wife got home from work.

Ina M. Griffin of Meadowbridge, W. V., a state known for its neighborliness and willingness to help folks anklet-deep in trouble. Ina wrote this: "I used to have the same trouble until I started pinning the pairs together with a safety pin before I put them in the washer. Never lose a sock now."

We're getting warmer, Ina. Problem is, if the B.W. can't find my socks, how can she keep track of where the safety pins are?

Then I received a rather more hefty envelope from Mrs.

R.M. Hazzard (I've lost her address). She wrote: "We had the same problem here until we found the Sox Locks or Sox Mates. They are the greatest and your B.W. will love you forever, if you use the locks every time you take your sox off." Also enclosed was a cardboard to which Mrs. Hazzard had taped a plastic ring with interior prongs through which you can pull a pair of socks, manufactured by a housewares outfit called Selfix, which is located in Chicago, where the Beautiful Wife grew up. Unfortunately not next to the Selfix factory.

Very, very good, Mrs. Hazzard. But not quite good enough. You forget that I'm a well-heeled (one blue, one brown) Grit columnist and thus have more than one pair of socks.

Then came a package from Vance R. Bettis of Lancaster, S. C., where I think many of my mismatched stockings were manufactured: "Dave, I was interested in your problem. . . . Since I used some of these, I have lost only three socks in five years."

"These" was an entire package of 24 sock mates by Selfix, more sock mates than I have pairs of socks unless you count the mismatched ones which I've already thrown away thanks to the advice from Paul Morin of Williamsport, Penn. And not only that! On the back of the package are very clear and specific directions about how to pull the socks (toes first) through the rings until the ring sits at the heels (both blue), in both English and Spanish. So now I don't even have to worry about a transfer to Acapulco.

~

# Chapter 5

# The B.W.

*Wyf is Mennes help & his confort,*
*His paradys terrestre and his disporte*
*—Geoffrey Chaucer*

WE'RE NOT QUITE finished with letters from readers yet. The first column in this chapter elicited more than 100 letters, more than for any other column I've ever written. Although the column was written five years ago, I still get letters from readers encouraging me to ignore a letter I received in 1983 from one Zoe Gouzally of Louisa, Va., concerning my wife and me.

What about my wife? Her name is Ruth Pirsig, I met her in graduate school, she's a wonderful teacher, scholar, musician, traveler, companion — and the Light of My Life.

Why I started referring to her in the column as B.W. (Beautiful Wife), I don't truly remember. I stopped for about a year after Zoe's suggestion, then resumed. I probably began originally because Ruth is my Wife and she is indeed Beautiful. And also because Grit readers — Zoe excluded — seem to enjoy my calling her that.

So here's a chapter of columns about my adventures and misadventures with B.W., including two hotel episodes, one of which almost resulted in her defenestration and the other of which resulted in my almost killing myself. See what an exciting life we lead?

# B.W. Lays an Egg

AS I'VE MENTIONED before, it's always great to get letters from Grit readers. I've had letters from people who tell me how to get my asparagus bed perking. I've had letters telling me the best way to eat bacon grease, letters wondering how my Beautiful Wife got lucky enough to land me and letters wondering how I got lucky enough to land her.

A thoughtful old gent from Michigan sent me a ceramic egg coddler when it became apparent that coddling was the only way I didn't know how to cook an egg. A kindly woman sent me a poster that says "God only made so many perfect heads. The rest he covered with hair." That poster has been hanging above my desk for about a year now.

I treasure all these missives, even the ones that are critical of what I have to say or how I say it. They are somehow special because I know the folks who send them have read my column carefully and care enough to send the very worst. Yesterday, I received such a letter from Zoe Gouzally of Louisa, Va. Here, in part, is what Zoe had to say:

"I enjoyed your column for a while but have just about quit reading it. The 'Beautiful Wife' bit is *not* interesting reading... In your column you can refer to her as 'The Mrs.' or 'my Wife,' but skip the Beautiful... Constantly repeating 'the Beautiful Wife' gives the impression that you are trying to convince *yourself.*"

By golly, Zoe, that's the last impression I want to make. I'm not so concerned about you out there in Louisa, Va. I'm concerned about right here in Minneapolis, in our kitchen. If, ah, The Mrs. ever got that impression, I'd be in some trouble. In my mind's eye I can see The Mrs. right now, peering across the top of Grit across the kitchen table.

"B.W., eh?" she'd say. "Are you sure, Dearest One, that those initials don't stand for Bow-Wow the dog?"

So my apologies, Zoe, for offending your considerable sensibilities. As I prepare to enter my third year as a columnist for Grit, the next to last thing I want to do is lose such a perceptive reader. I guess I got started, Zoe, with the B.W. business because all the columnists up in these parts have code names for their spouses. Columnist Robert T. Smith always refers to his wife as "She Who Must Be Obeyed." Our colleague at the Star Tribune, columnist Larry Batson, refers to his wife as "A Woman I Know Very Well." S.W.M.B.O and A.W.I.K.V.W. I guess I just thought B.W. would be a short and snappy way to refer to The Mrs.

The Mrs. is very beautiful, with auburn hair, big almond eyes and a figure so lithe that last spring she was able to slide into the dress she wore at her sister's wedding 25 years ago, when she was 12. (The Mrs. was 12, not her sister.) So it never occurred to me that she might think I had to convince myself of her charms by using the Beautiful Wife business again and again in a national publication.

But after pondering your letter, I've concluded that your remarks are reasonable. Once in a while The Mrs. worries about her nose, which she thinks is too long. And her feet, which she thinks are too big. And her arms, which she thinks are too thin.

So maybe I'd better cool it. But I won't call her S.N. for Ski Nose or B.F. for Big Foot. Or T.P.A. for Toothpick Arms. I'll just call her Ruth, because that's her name, a beautiful name to match her beautiful self. OK?

And as for you, Zoe, I'm going to call you P.R., Perceptive Reader, for the way you ended your letter. "My best wishes to you both. I get the impression that you love her. God Bless." God bless you, P.R.

(*Author's note:* The letters poured in, mostly from women who said they wished their husbands would refer to them as B.W. and I wouldn't *dare* to keep my promise to Zoe. So I weakened. For a year, I referred to Ruth as the Wife who is Beautiful [W.B.], just to keep the letter of my promise to Zoe intact. Not good enough, as the letters continued to come. So I flat out broke my promise and returned to B.W, as explained in the following column. I haven't heard from Zoe since.)

～

# Name Controversy Effects Change

DEAR WIFE who is Beautiful: Gee, W.B., that's an awkward salutation, isn't it? Now that the Valentine Season is upon us, I felt constrained to drop you a note to tell you that after knowing you 18 years, you're more beautiful than ever, but that I simply must stop referring to you as W.B. in my Grit column.

Remember the good old days, when I called you B.W.? That's something everyone could understand after the first reference. Then Zoe from Virginia wrote and said that she thought I did protest too much, that if you were really beautiful I wouldn't have to say so. So I made a promise in that estimable publication, W.B., that I wouldn't call you B.W. anymore. And I haven't.

Not calling you B.W., W.B., has caused all sorts of problems for me. After I made the promise, scores of letters came in advising me that I was a coward for not sticking to my convictions, that they liked B.W. better than W.B. One person wrote to say that whenever she saw the initials she thought of a Wet Bat. Others accused me of backing out of a perfectly decent term of endearment.

And remember how those letters bothered you, in your modesty? I thought for a time of calling you B.M.W. (Beautiful, Modest Wife), but then I figured some reader from West Germany would confuse you with that expensive automobile. So I just stuck with the new nomenclature, W.B., W.B. Problem was, that every time I used it, I felt constrained to explain to readers that it means Wife who is Beautiful, which ate up a lot of newsprint in Williamsport, Pa.

Finally, I've mustered up courage and am going to break my promise to the fine woman who originally complained about the original. From now on, you're B.W. in my book and in Grit, too. I can't bear to confuse you with a bat or a foreign car and I don't like to see vast stands of timber cut down to make room for the substitute.

Back to Valentine's Day, B.W., and my message to you:
From *Sonnets to the Peachy Kid, My Wife.*

*How do I love thee? Let me count the ways.*
*I love thee to the depth and breadth and height*
*My midsection can reach, after eating all in sight,*
*Your curry of lamb, apple and bays.*
*I love thee to the extent that every day's*
*A romp, Italy sun or winter light.*
*I love thee freely, as flies the April kite;*
*I love thee purely, as thee turns from Praise,*
*When you sing in church old Lutheran lays,*
*Or minister to the grief of forgotten souls.*
*I love thee with a love I seemed to lose*
*With misspent youth — I love thee with the breath,*
*Short now, of all my life! — and, if God choose*
*I shall love thee better after I can start referring to you as*
*B.W. again.*

Well, B.W., there you have it. It ain't much, but I never promised you a rose garden nor did I claim that I was any relation to Elizabeth Barrett Browning.

You're my peachy kid, B.W., peachy because you're a peach and your maiden name is Pirsig, which loosely translated means "peach." Come to think of it, maybe I could call you the P.W. No, I guess I'll stick with the old favorite.

~

# Wood's Sensible Guide for the Married Man

**W**HEN RUTH, my Wife Who Is Beautiful — no kidding she really is, I'm not just trying to convince myself, her or anyone, no, no kidding — when she announced that she and her mother were taking a 10-day tour of the East Coast I said to her, "Boy, will I miss you, honey."

And then I thought to myself, "Will it ever be great to have the house all to myself. Just think of the things I could do once out from under her ever-watchful gaze!"

I would eat popcorn for supper every night. With lots of salt, not the substitute stuff that tastes like water softener. I would leave socks strewn all over the house and cupboard doors open. I could watch sleazy TV sitcoms clad only in my boxer shorts, with my bare feet up on the coffee table and empty Diet Pepsi bottles lined up like sentinels around my easy chair. Oh sure, and I'd take in a couple Twins games with the guys, we'd joke around and not worry about getting home for dinner or even a midnight snack. We'd have a ball. And I'd snore every night — z-z-z-z-z! — without a jab in the ribs from You Know Who.

As you may have suspected by now, I'm something of a slob. And Ruth, well, she's the woman who always cleans the house before the cleaning lady comes on Thursdays.

So it would be glorious. No regular mealtimes. Just make a peanut butter and pink bologna sandwich whenever I felt like it. I'd eat it out on the deck and look at the sun sinking behind the big pine tree next door. No one around to ask where our next dollar was coming from or whether we should buy a new cook- stove or would I please shovel the cobwebs out of my personal shower in the basement.

As it turned out, I was only about half right and that was the wrong half.

I bade her farewell at the airport, then hopped in the car and drove to my new-found freedom. The first night was glorious. I popped a big kettle of corn, salted it liberally and washed it down with a liter or two of Diet Pepsi while watching "Eight is Enough," and an aged movie about World War II commandoes. At 11 p.m., I threw my socks under, and me into, the bed, where I polished off a quarter-pound of saltines with peanut butter and onions, while reading my latest copy of Grit.

And then I slept. When I awoke, I hoped I had snored, but didn't know because there was no one around to poke me in the ribs.

After work the next day, I found that no one was available for a baseball outing. So I went home and sat on the deck, which was awfully quiet, awfully somber. The pink bologna sandwich turned to ashes in my mouth, so I turned in early. I tossed and turned all night, wondering where our next dollar was coming from and whether or not we should buy a new cookstove. I must have dozed off at 3 a.m., then awoke and went to work groggy.

Night after night passed without the Wife Who Is Beautiful. Folks who had promised to drop by called to say there was a funeral in the family or they had tickets to a concert and, gee, we'll have to get together some time.

On the weekend, I shoveled the cobwebs out of my personal shower in the basement. Then I closed the cupboard doors and dug the socks from under the bed and did the laundry. On Saturday night, I sat in my shorts in front of the tube, and ate popcorn that tasted like water softener. I figured I wanted to live long enough to see Ruth upon her return.

Three days later, she returned and these days I'm sleeping very well thank you. Except when I get a jab in the ribs from her needle-y elbow.

~

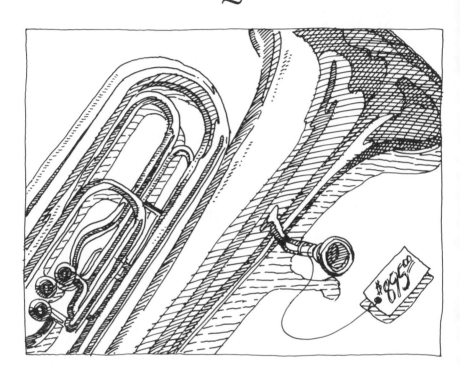

## B.W.: *Golddigger of 1983*

**M**Y **BEAUTIFUL WIFE** is Always Right. She's not the pushy sort, understand, who harps away about being right all the time or saying I told you so or don't you beat all! Oh, no. She just sort of gracefully glides through life, Being Right.

A year and a half ago, I bought a junker tuba with more dents than a '56 Chevy at a demolition derby. It served me well, but as I regained my proficiency, I wanted to upgrade. So I got in touch with instrument saleswoman Bonnie Hill and she got to looking around for a horn with fewer dents.

Now, I'm no big spender, but I realized that modern alloy instruments aren't exactly cheap. So I figured I'd pay up to $1,500 bucks (that's a lot of Grit columns) for some fairly new tuba that had been kicked around and dropped down stairs for only a few years by high school boys deemed unfit for trumpets or oboes or glockenspiels. About a month ago, saleswoman Hill called and said, "Dave, I've got just the horn for you. There aren't too many dents, it's relatively small, light, we'll throw the carrying cases in free. *And it's only 895 dollars.*"

My wheels never touched the pavement in my 20-mile trip to the suburban music store. I'm here to tell you that my newish tuba is beauteous, its conformation so modern, so efficient that you couldn't get more than 10 or 12 hogsheads of a mad Bavarian King's finest claret poured into its tubing.

So I bought the horn from Bonnie Hill and brought it home to show the B.W., an accomplished singer and pianist and a person who specializes in baroque music and always Being Right. B.W. liked my new horn at first blare. Her instrument is a Steinway studio model piano with no dents. She asked how much money. I told her $895.

She said, "That's not enough. That horn's probably no good. You should have spent twice as much. Why are you so cheap?" I brushed her critique aside and sat down to run through my special rendition of "Asleep in the Deep."

Things went well until last Tuesday, when I went to band rehearsal. B.W. came along to sing with the band a new tune written especially for her by poet Steve Alnes. It's called "The Last Word in Wisconsin is Sin." Well, we never got to that because valve No. 1 on my $895 tuba was stuck tighter than a cork in a Methodist's jug of bourbon. If I pressed the piston down into the cylinder, it wouldn't come up. If I pried it up, it wouldn't go down.

B.W. sat on the sidelines, looking at me in wry bemusement. We left rehearsal tuneless and on the morn she offered to take it to a music shop for repair. That night I returned from work and there sat the tuba, gleaming in its stand. Valve No. 1 went up and down sst-sst.

"Oh, gee, B.W. thank you, thank you," I said. "What was wrong with it?"

"Your cheap tuba has fiberglass guides implanted in the valves. No. 1 guide was flattened out and the man had to file it narrower."

"Oh. How much did that cost?"

"Oh," said B.W. "About $2,500."

"$2,500! Just to file down a guide!?"

"Well," said B.W. "Not exactly. He filed the guide for nothing. But while I was waiting for him, I wandered into the piano department. And I found this wonderful Kawai baby grand piano marked down. The salesman said I could have it for my Steinway and just $2,500 extra. I think I should do it. What do you think?"

What could I say? The B.W. is Always Right.

~

# D.W., B.W. And The P.

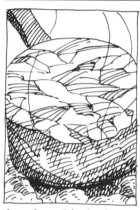

A FEW WEEKS back, I fell in love with a pot. No, not *pot* pot, not grass, not Tiajuana Gold, not marijuana. What I fell in love with was a metal pot, something in which people cooked soup before the Era of Campbell. Earlier I wrote about the ritzy Empress Hotel in Victoria, B.C., where the Beautiful Wife and I spent part of Christmas vacation. The next stop on our voyage was to be a log cabin at Kalaloch Lodge on the Washington seacoast. We'd been told that the cabin had a cookstove, but no cooking utensils. So one day we sneaked out of the Empress and made our way to Victoria's Goodwill store. We needed a pot to heat water in. We found one for a dollar at the Goodwill.

I liked the looks of that pot even before we smuggled it into the Empress. It was old, to be sure, and had lost the lustre it had when a Canadian housewife had purchased it new, maybe 30 years ago. It was a four-quart pot. It had a wooden handle on top and a metal handle on the side for pouring. It had something I'd never seen before: Opposite the metal handle, about two inches down from the rim, there was a tiny pouring spout. With such a spout, you could drain water off spaghetti without strands flopping into the sink.

And so it was that I left the Empress and headed for the harsh, driftwood-strewn Pacific coast and our Christmas cabin, armed with aluminum foil to cook our rolled roast, my beloved wife and my beloved pot.

Our Christmas cabin at Kalaloch Lodge was beautiful. A

brass bed, a fireplace and a box of firewood, a refrigerator, hot and cold running water, even a stack of evergreen boughs from which the B.W. fashioned a Christmas tree. One thing was lacking. There was a stove, but it didn't have an oven. As I put the magnificent rolled roast into the refrigerator, I wondered how we could prepare it without an oven. But not to worry. We had two days to think of that. Meanwhile the wonderful old pot served as a coffee maker, as an object of great beauty and as the utensil in which we cooked traditional oyster stew on Christmas Eve, as the logs in the fireplace merrily crackled.

The B.W. gave me a lovely set of dominoes that night and as we reintroduced ourselves to that pleasant old game, I kept wondering about the morrow and that dratted traditional rolled roast. Perhaps we could take a lesson from Attila the Hun, who cooked his roasts by tying them to the flank of his horse and racing it up and down the steppes until it was warm. One problem: no horses. Perhaps, perhaps.

Christmas Day dawned and it came to me, a genuine epiphany. I sprang from my chair, grabbed the pot and a roll of foil. As I browned the roast in the pot, I rolled tight several strips of foil into two inch balls. I removed the roast, put the foil balls in the pot's bottom, then gently placed the roast on top of them. Later, I got a roaring fire going. I sealed the top of the pot with foil and set it on the red hot coals. Then I prayed. Would the wonderful old pot survive, or would it melt in the blast furnace and turn our roast to a cinder?

An hour later, I gingerly retrieved the pot from its fiery resting place. I opened it and my prayers were answered. The meat was medium rare and toothsome. Who needed a convection oven when you had a pot like this?

When we left to catch our plane in Seattle the next day, I wanted to take the old pot along. It fit nowhere but in the trash can outside the cabin. That hurt. Driving to Seattle, I wondered about the old pot. Had it belonged to a French woman, who cooked lovely ragouts for her *mari bien-aimé*? Or to someone of English descent, who overcooked cabbage in it every day? Whoever owned it before, I'm certain it served them.

～

# By the Shores of Lake Nokomis

**A** FEW MONTHS back, the Beautiful Wife and I put our bicycles in mothballs and took up just plain walking to see if I could soften up my ancient arteries. For years, we pedaled around Lake Nokomis on our Huffys almost every night. But I tired of the routine and one day I set out on foot.

That took an hour, rather than 30 minutes on wheels. But the walk was more fun. Traveling at a slower pace, I began to see magnificent old trees I'd missed, heard the waters of the lake lap up to the shore. There was time to make a smiling face for the faces that I met. So now it's a walk almost every afternoon for B.W. and me, a walk that lets us talk over the day past and the days to come.

Last Thursday, B.W. had to give Danny Monaghan his piano lesson, so I set out by myself. It was cool and gloomy by the lake and when I got to 50th St. and Woodlawn Blvd., I thought I'd make a detour and visit old friend Harold Emery Geiger, the Sweet Singer of Nokomis. It had been a year since I had written about him for Grit. Geiger is the 84-year-old who writes poems that actually rhyme, poems written in the meter of Longfellow and other writers he studied as a kid growing up on the shores of Nokomis.

I climbed the hill to his brick house and wondered how the year had treated him and if the octogenarian could still hear a doorbell. Before I turned the corner to his front lawn, I saw a cloud of dust rising above his steeply slanted lawn and heard the whoosh-whoosh-whooshing of a bamboo rake.

I turned the corner and there was Harold Emery Geiger all bundled up with a floppy wool stocking cap perched atop his snowy mane. The Sweet Singer of Nokomis was raking up a storm. We talked for a time of the beautiful trees on his front lawn, trees he'd dug up elsewhere and planted on the lawn of the first home he ever built.

Would I like to come in and chat for a spell? You bet. Harold Emery Geiger huffed and puffed up the hill and we entered his pleasant living room.

He told me that after the article in Grit appeared, readers from 20 states and two territories had ordered his book of verse,

"From the Mountains to the Prairies." In fact, he'd just sold out the first printing and had made enough money to get him thinking about publishing the autobiography he's working on.

"Of course, I'm so busy with everything else," he smiled, "that I don't know when I'll finish the manuscript."

Busy with senior citizen groups, with bowling and with visiting his son and daughter whenever he can scrape up the time.

Harold Emery Geiger likes to keep busy because it's lonely for him and his dog, Champ. His wife, Alice, died nine years ago and the modest house they shared for so many years is quiet. A few years ago, he penned the following poem about the passing of Alice:

> *The sun will shine; the wind will blow,*
> *The passing years will come and go*
> *And very few will ever know*
> *That she is gone.*
> *Where e'er I look, I see her face;*
> *I miss the warmth of her embrace;*
> *No one can ever take her place*
> *And she is gone.*
> *I hear her footsteps on the stair*
> *And rush to see if she is there,*
> *But all I find is empty air,*
> *For she is gone.*
> *For me, the birds no longer sing;*
> *For me, no summer, fall or spring;*
> *She was my all, my everything.*
> *And she is gone.*

I re-read his tribute to a woman I never knew, bade Harold Emery Geiger adieu, then hurried home to my beautiful wife, thankful. Very thankful.

~

# Weddings Aren't What They Used to Be

**A** **FEW WEEKS** back, I had the great pleasure to spend a day with two seniors at Aitkin High School, in northern Minnesota. I went to class with them, ate hot lunch with them, chatted with their friends. They were wholesome, well-scrubbed kids, who didn't say "you know" three times per sentence. They participate in all kinds of sports, work part-time, sing in the school choir, want to attend college next year. I hope they make it, because with kids like them, our country's future is more secure than some naysayers would have it.

The boy was Chris Midthun and the girl was Roxie McGillis. The last class we attended together was called "Marriage and Parenthood." Roxie explained that the purpose of the course was to prepare students for the realities of marriage and the arrival of children. Not a bad idea. When I graduated from high school I figured my whole marriage would resemble a scene from "Life with Father."

Roxie and Chris were excited about the class because on this day they would get married to each other, then eat cake and drink punch that the teacher, Mrs. Mathson, had brought for the occasion. In fact, *all* the kids in class were getting married that day. When the mock nuptials were over, Roxie and Chris handed in their day's written assignment. And what might that be?

"Oh, it's a detailed budget of our wedding and honeymoon costs," said Roxie brightly.

And how much might that add up to?

"It adds up to $19,850.00," said Roxie without a flutter from those beautiful long lashes.

"Isn't that a bit steep?" I asked. "Couldn't you have eloped and taken the money and put a down payment on a condo?"

"Well," said Roxie, "it's not cheap to get married. My dress cost $900 and we're honeymooning in the Bahamas. But I *did* try to economize. Chris's tux only costs $40 (watch out for this girl, Chris) and our dance will be at the Legion Hall, which is much cheaper than renting the Armory."

Later that week, I talked to Roxie's mother, Linda, who

thought back 20 years and said her wedding to Roxie's father cost "about $300."

Linda is my kind of woman. And so is my wife, Ruth. We were married in 1970, soon after we got out of graduate school and landed our first teaching jobs. Money was tight and so was I. Ruth, God bless her, played along and we came in with the World's Cheapest Wedding Outside Scotland's Borders.

First, we needed a place to get married. The tiny chapel at Augsburg College was free and so that was it. Then, we needed someone to marry us. Who better than my friend Dr. Douglas Ollila, an ordained minister who occupied the office next to me at Augsburg? Oh, and we had to have music. Why not select some 18th-century religious music from my album collection and let my roommate Sherman Johnsrud operate a portable phonograph borrowed from the school's audio visual department? Why not, indeed? Ruth lived in an apartment presentable enough for a reception.

So the night before our wedding we made our way to all the grocery sales in town, then worked late into the night concocting finger sandwiches and dips and such.

The wedding went off with few hitches. After our guests had their fill of cheap cream-cheese sandwiches, we headed off for our opulent honeymoon. Two nights at the St. Paul Hotel, the nation's best reason for urban renewal. Seventeen bucks a night. And when we returned to work on Monday, we still didn't have a down payment on a condo. Maybe Roxie McGillis had the right idea.

~

## The Defenestration of St. Paul

**H**ERE COMES MY third annual column about our wedding anniversary. It was perfect. Unless you count the fact Ruth almost fell out of our hotel room window onto the street nine stories below. Time magazine would have called her death "by defenestration."

But let's start at the beginning. As I've mentioned before, our wedding in 1970 occurred under circumstances that could be best described as flat broke. We got married in the chapel where I taught because it was free. We made our own hors' d'oeuvres for our reception. And then there was the problem of a hotel for our two-day honeymoon. I called every hotel in downtown Minneapolis, all of whom asked $35 a night, which would have shot the entire honeymoon budget.

Then I made a chance phone call across the Mississippi to the St. Paul Hotel. They wanted $17 a night. Hey now. That was more like it. So I reserved a room in that old landmark in the Saintly City of Landmarks. We arrived there after the reception. The old landmark had seen better days. The old Gopher Grill, which had entertained so many celebrities in the past, was empty, cavernous.

Our room was in a sad state of repair, but it served its purpose and we spent a joyous weekend, with me opening my paper-thin wallet whenever hunger pangs got unbearable. On Monday morning, we had a dollar left for gas to get back across the river.

Well, the years have come and gone and life has been good to Ruth and me. So now when the anniversary rolls around, we pay tribute to that good fortune by doing something lavish. Last year, the Lincoln hotel chain bought the ragged old St. Paul Hotel. They gussied it up with limo service, a beautiful lobby, a four-star French restaurant to replace the old Gopher Grill and they redid the shabby rooms. Guess where we stayed on our wedding anniversary?

But the night before that, we started our celebration by attending a wonderful concert of 18th-century music featuring the world's greatest oboist, Switzerland's Heinz Holliger. Some may say, "18th-century music? Yechh! Oboe soloist? Phooey!" But in my view, any music written after the 18th century is too far out.

As for oboes, sometimes they can sound like the neighborhood bully strangling a cat. But not Heinz Holliger's oboe. Holliger, who looks like a cross between Mr. Peepers and the Road Runner, can make an oboe sound like the voices of an angelic choir.

So you can see how our anniversary got off to a perfect start. On the following day we drove up to the elegant St. Paul Hotel, a valet parked our elegant Dodge Colt, and we checked in. Waiting for us in our spiffy new room were 14 long-stemmed red roses, sent over by our friends Robert and Janet Smith, who, if they don't watch their own pocketbooks, will never be able to afford going out on their own wedding anniversary. We repaired to Etoile, the fancy dining room, where we feasted for the better part of the evening. We turned in early.

At about 4 a.m., I awoke in the monstrous bed and reached over to pat Ruth's lovely auburn locks. No locks. No Ruth. Where could that kid be? I sat up in bed. I looked to my left and there was my spouse, lying draped across a wing chair and a table, her head out the window, sleeping peacefully. When she awoke, she explained that she was roused at 1 a.m. by intense heat. She turned the thermostat down to 20 below, but the heat kept coming, so she opened the window and slept partially outside.

Nothing in the world, folks, is perfect. But we tried to look on the bright side. Fourteen years ago the windows in the St. Paul Hotel probably would have been painted shut.

~

## Student Affairs

**W**HEN I CAME HOME from work, I knew there was trouble. Ruth's German jaw stuck out about an inch further than normal and her eyeballs were spinning in their sockets.

"What, my Beautiful One," asked I, "is troubling you?"

"Never mind," she spluttered. "I'll tell you on our walk."

So off we went on our daily walk around Lake Nokomis, with me running at full tilt just to keep up, hoping that I was not the unconscious agent of her red-hot disposition.

When we came to the spot where the dead carp was decomposing, Ruth spilled her anguish on the shores. Seems that the day before she had taken her eighth-grade English class to a special presentation on computers. She left the presentation for a few minutes and when she returned she found her class had left the presentation and was in the hallway break dancing. You know break dancing, the new fad where you spin on your head and do all kinds of physically impossible gyrations. Well, Ruth thinks that break dancing is just great, but not proper activity when kids are supposed to be learning about computers so they can beat us old folks out of jobs as soon as they turn 18.

So she disciplined them. Tsk, tsk.

She told them they had an option. They could stay after school for 15 minutes. (She's a tough cookie.) Or, if they chose not to stay after school, they could go home and write the sentence "I will treat education with more respect in the future" 200 times.

Some kids stayed after school; others chose the writing option. On the following morning, most kids handed in their punishments and went about their business. Not a young lass we'll call Little Miss Petulant. She came in with no sentences and a letter from her mommy, whom we'll call Mrs. Sheltering Arms.

Mrs. Arms wrote Ruth that she had taught school and was Up On All The Current Educational Theory and that it was unconscionable of Ruth to make such a barbaric assignment, that it served no educational purpose and, besides, little Miss Petulant had to miss her favorite TV show to complete it.

In the class that morning, Little Miss Petulant had a partner.

Little Miss Smartypants. She didn't have her sentences either. "Why not?" asked Ruth.

"Because I agree with Mrs. Sheltering Arm's letter," said the eighth-grader, who was also Up On All The Current Educational Theory.

Oh boy-oh-boy.

I remembered the days when I was in junior high. If I threw soap erasers, I had to miss the Jack Benny show, my favorite, so I could write "I'll never throw erasers again" 1,000 times on my Rainbow tablet. But I never brought it up to Ma and Pa. If I had, their punishment would have been swift, sure and I'd have had trouble sitting at my desk the next day. If a teacher cracked me across the chops for goofing off in the cloak hall, that wasn't mentioned either, lest Pa ask me to turn the other cheek. Of course, all this abuse scarred me for life. If you don't believe it, look at the record. Year after year, they pass me up for the presidential nomination of either party. Year after year, I never get even a Pulitzer Prize honorable mention. I'm a wreck.

I told Ruth of my concern as we walked past the ducks waddling along the bay. I worried aloud about the emotional trauma she had probably caused Miss Petulant. And then Ruth told me she wouldn't be teaching next year and pushed me into Minnehaha Creek.

~

## *In the Storm of The Teeth*

**T**HIS IS GOING to be a tale told by an idiot, full of sound and fury, signifying something. I don't know what.

As your tale-teller today, I'm the idiot. And I'm full of sound and fury because of what happened a few weeks back. The late news was over and I was performing ritual ablutions before turning in for the night. Ruth was tidying up, which means sweeping up crumbs I've left during several trips to the kitchen during TV commercial breaks. I stood in the doorway admiring her as she flipped on the garbage disposal.

"Bang-bang-bang-clackety-clackety-clack," said the disposal.

"My goodness," exclaimed Ruth. "There must be a teaspoon down there."

I knew instinctively there was no teaspoon down there. She's seldom wrong, but this time I could feel her error. I could feel it in my jaw. Or should I say I could feel its absence in my jaw?

You guessed it. My lovely wife had just ground up my partial plate, those four little fake lower teeth that had chewed me through life so faithfully for almost 15 years. I had foolishly put them in a water glass at sinkside, rather than the plastic container they belonged in. And I had forgotten them as a drowsy numbness overtook me.

I reached down into the disposal's innards and dragged up a mangled piece of stainless steel and some mysterious synthetic that had served me so well. Perhaps now would be a good time to go on a diet, thought I. It will take at least a week to fabricate new ones and, like fellow Grit columnist Mike Cummings, I get very bored with oatmeal after half a cupful.

The next day, I called Painless Loyle Raymond, my trusty dentist. Dr. Raymond, in his most diplomatic voice, said, "You did *what?* Oh. You'd better come in right away."

What was the hurry, wondered I, as I made my way to his chrome and porcelain office. I've been putting off this diet for a long time and he'll have my new choppers before I lost the requisite 50 pounds.

The hurry, explained the Dentist with the Delicate Touch, is that he would have to build the partial from scratch. This construction project would require at least six calls, spaced out so the construction crew at the lab could do their fabricating.

Dental technician Barbara Pfaffe, who has cleaned my real teeth for years, stopped laughing long enough to tell me she'd heard some rare stories about what happens to people's dentures. "But I never heard anyone grinding them up in a *garbage disposal!*"

Then Barbara broke back into paroxysms of laughter. I made my second appointment, then went to work. That night, I broke my diet and took Ruth to a lovely new restaurant in town. I took my first bite of steamed mussels. "Bang-bang-bang-clackety-clackety-clack," said a molar.

The lovely new restaurant's chef had failed to remove a mussel shell from the tender bivalve into which I had bitten. The molar upon which one side of my old partial had rested broke into two pieces. Apparently the metal clamp that had wound around the molar had saved me from the same fate for years. So it was back to the Painless Loyle Raymond. He wearily looked into my gaping maw. He shook his head.

"You'll need a crown for this molar. And as long as we're at it, we should crown the other tooth that supports the molar. That's in bad shape, too. So when you leave make four more appointments."

The fury has passed. But the sound lingers on, the sound of hot air whistling between my two lower canines.

~

# Music Appreciation

UP HERE IN MINNEAPO-LIS, everything is wonderful. We have a wonderful symphony orchestra, a wonderful hall for it to perform in. Outside that hall we have Peavey Plaza, a wonderful promenade with shrubbery and a big pond, a place for lovers to stroll around, for office workers to take their lunch, a place for people who like simple elegance.

At least that's what I thought Peavey Plaza was for until last night when the Beautiful Wife and I attended the first concert of our subscription series. Now I know what Peavey Plaza is *really* for.

Let's back up a bit. As you might have heard, Minnesota is a state with lots of Scandinavians. Nothing wrong with Scandinavians, mind you. I have some Viking blood coursing through my veins and I'm proud of it. But I'll have to admit that modern Scandinavian-Americans don't have much in common with those early ancestors who plundered and pillaged and made a lot of noise. The most noise you'll get out of modern Scandinavians usually comes from their Lutheran church choirs.

Scandinavians up here are modest and polite in the extreme. They don't wear their emotions on their sleeves, if you get my drift. There's the old story of the Norwegian husband who loved his wife so much that once he almost told her so. Back in the '60s, students up here usually asked permission of the dean before they staged demonstrations. Scandinavians never come right out and say something, but sort of back into a conversation. I remember an old man who came into my parents' restaurant out of a 40-below-zero cold snap. His first remark? "I *wonder* if it's cold out?"

The best word to describe Scandinavians in Minnesota is "seemly."

OK. Back to Orchestra Hall the other night. We got up into our cheap balcony seats, which were so high that I started feeling light-headed. We looked at our programs and found to our dismay that this 2½-hour concert was to consist entirely of Russian and Finnish music. Twentieth-century Russian and Finnish music. Not our cup of tea, which we prefer brewed in a modest Mozartian pot rather than in a samovar. We've got nothing against Russians or Finns. We just don't particularly care for their 20th-century music.

We sat through Shostakovich's Symphony in F Minor, Opus 10. This piece sounded not unlike our young neighbor boy trying to scare a fox out of a hen house by blowing mighty blasts on the trumpet his parents just bought him. Then on to a piece by Kokkonen, etc., etc. Intermission finally came with a promise of Mussorgsky and Prokofiev after the break. The B.W. leaned over to me and said, "Let's leave."

Leave? The B.W. had never suggested such a course of concert activity in 15 years of wedded bliss. Worse yet, would it be polite, would it be Scandinavian, would it be *seemly* to leave in the middle of a concert? And would conductor Neville Marriner be offended if he found out? Oh, shucks. Let's live dangerously.

So we crept down five flights of stairs onto the main floor. Everyone seemed to be watching us. So I said to B.W., "Let's catch a breath of fresh air out on that wonderful Peavey Plaza."

And B.W. said, "What a wonderful idea."

And so we stepped out on Peavey Plaza, where other concertgoers chatted and gazed out on the shimmering pool. We gazed and chatted, and carefully walked backward — sort of like Michael Jackson — until we were at our parking lot two blocks away. And then we drove the back streets home.

~

# Mid-Century

**W**ELL IT'S FINALLY happened. I've turned 50. Five decades short of a century. Ten decades shy of my sesquicentennial.

But if you think I'm going to complain, think again. I'm happy to be here.

Not all my friends who hit the mid-century mark have done so as graciously as I'm doing today.

One friend turned 50 last year and stayed in bed for the better part of six months, sucking his thumb and reading old Batman comic books.

Another left his wife and family and ran off with a stewardess from Omaha.

Still another complained of illness constantly. His wife said this: "I've had to put my foot down. I don't let him watch reruns of Ben Casey anymore. Doctor Kildare is OK, but Ben Casey sends him into a dither."

How so?

"Well, he thinks he's catching the disease that these TV doctors happen to be treating on a given day. Ben Casey does a lot of brain surgery, subdermal hematomas and like that. Well, when that happens, he starts holding his head, imagines sharp pains in the cranium and begins to act real crazy. But Doctor Kildare? He's just a general practitioner. I can put up with a husband who thinks he's got a stomach ache. But a brain tumor? No way!"

I can't figure out guys like that.

If it's true that life begins at 40, we must just be hitting our stride at 50. That makes sense, doesn't it? Doesn't it? You bet it does.

Fifty feels good on me. I've noticed a spring in my step this morning that I didn't have yesterday when I was 49. I was even hungry for breakfast. Ate two eggs and bacon and got no indigestion for my troubles. I looked in the mirror for gray hair along the fringe.

"Not a one!" I shouted to the B.W., who is only 40, but has numerous silver threads among her gold.

"Don't be so certain," she cautioned. "You have blonde hair — what there is of it, hee hee — and gray hair can hide behind it."

So what? I've still got that spring in my step.

As I examined my face for wrinkles — not a one — and thanked whatever god who made me for my ability to face 50 with grace and style, the B.W. called her mother in Chicago. I listened in on the upstairs phone:

"David's 50 today, Mom."

"Oh, gosh, I forgot his card. How's he taking it?"

"Amazingly well, Mom. You know how nuts he can be?"

"Yes, I certainly do. I'll never forget the time he couldn't get a piece of shell off an egg he was frying. Remember? He broke all the eggshells into the pan and stirred them around."

"Mom, how could I forget? But he's taking this amazingly well."

"Funny," said B.M.I.L. (Beautiful Mother-in-Law). "I've heard of men who take to their bed with Batman comics, men who run off with younger women. . . . "

"But not David, Mom. I wonder why he's responding so well to this when he reacts so violently to everything else. Remember when he spilled the can of paint. . . . "

Finally, I broke into the conversation. "The explanation of why I'm taking this like a man, ladies, is simple."

"How so?" they chorused.

"I've felt like I'm 50 since I was 20. So it's no big adjustment."

∼

# B.W., No Polka Partner

**A**BOUT A YEAR AGO I told you how I had reached the half-century mark in my life and that my Beautiful Wife had complimented me on taking this event so calmly and evenhandedly. I explained that reaching 50 years of age was no big deal to me because I had felt as if I were 50 since I was 20.

Well, today I feel very, very old and despondent. That's not because one whole year has intervened since I last wrote on the subject of my age. I'm feeling very, very old and despondent today because of what happened yesterday.

It all began when the B.W. persuaded me to take her to see a movie in downtown Minneapolis. We arrived at Hennepin Av. 20 minutes early.

Next door to the Skyway Theater is a record and tapes store called Musicland. B.W. was surprised when I quickly agreed to enter this establishment for a few minutes before buying our movie tickets.

She didn't know I had a motive in mind. I planned to buy as many tapes as I could afford to play on the excellent tape deck that came with our new car. Was I on the prowl for some Beethoven or Bach, Mozart or Mendelssohn? Not on your life! You see, I was nurtured in western Wisconsin, the Cradle of Polkadom. There's nothing I like better than hearing the rat-a-tat-tat of a good cornetist, the tweedles of two German or Polish clarinetists backed up by the ooms and the pahs of my favorite instrument, the tuba, which I play myself with little facility.

Ah, I could already hear it. I'd be driving alone somewhere up north and blasting through the car's four speakers would be the strains of "The Schneider Polka" or the syncopated beat of the "Johann Pa Schnippen" schottische.

B.W. headed for the classical section as I stood there, surrounded by tattered kids with safety pins poked through their earlobes, sporting spiky punk haircuts that made them look as if they'd just seen the ghost of John Lennon. They browsed as my old eardrums adjusted to the din coming from countless overhead speakers.

The sight of row after row of rock and acid rock record bins assaulted my bifocals and I was about to give up on my quest for the stylings of Whoopee John Wilfahrt, my culture hero, and Harold Loefflemacher and his Six Fat Dutchmen. Both Wilfahrt and Loefflemacher hailed from New Ulm, Minn., often billed as "The Polka Capital of the World." It was pretty obvious that New Ulm was not well represented here at Musicland.

But wait! Off to the side of the cavernous store, toward the back, was a sign above one small bin. It said, simply, "Old Time." I waddled over and started riffling through. Glenn Miller. Benny Goodman. Artie Shaw. This was "old time"? Not where I came from. Miller, Goodman and Shaw played music for big city folks. Old time where I came from was Loefflemacher, Wilfahrt, Lawrence Duchow and his Red Raven Orchestra. Shucks.

Meanwhile, over in "Classical," B.W. was browsing and what did she find? Two tapes, one of the Whoopee John orchestra and one of The Six Fat Dutchmen, snuggled up against Bach and Beethoven. Sure, sure, they're all Germans, but I never thought of "She's Too Fat for Me," as being classical music, or even semi-classical. But I snatched up the tapes and said, "Let's go to the movie," to which B.W. replied: "I'm not walking through the checkout with you if you're going to buy those. Let me get out of here before you go through."

Once B.W. was on the street, I sheepishly slid the tapes and $8 across the counter. The 18-year-old clerk looked in wonderment. "Ah, er, I'm from New Ulm," said I. He probably thought that was just a little south of Mars.

～

# B.W., A Real Rib Tickler

**H**ERE'S A RIB TICKLER for you. Well, not exactly.

When you read this, the Beautiful Wife and I will have spent 17 years of wedded bliss. It's a near-perfect match by all accounts. Near-perfect, not perfect. This fly in the ointment that salves our hearts, this grit in the ball bearing that makes our daily life go 'round, this cockroach in the ice cube of the sweet and effervescent punch bowl that is our marriage, I regret to report, is all my fault.

I snore. And B.W. can't sleep when I do it.

B.W. could tolerate certain types of snores, but she can't tolerate mine. She could tolerate, she says, the Whistle Snore, which goes s-s-s-s-s s-s-s-s-s s-s-s-s-s. Notice that there are five lo-o-ong s's between each pause.

"If you'd only snore in a regular rhythm, a predictable way, I could get used to that," says B.W., "and I could eventually fall asleep."

That makes sense. I once had the indistinct honor of sharing a motel room with Dick Caldwell, my friend who tells the joke about the pig so smart the farmer didn't want to butcher him all at one time. Caldwell's snore sounds like 64 steel-wheeled hay wagons rumbling down a cobblestone street that winds its way through a tunnel.

How, thought I, will I ever get to sleep? But within an hour, I was acclimated to Caldwell's gasps, which were as regular as a metronome, and I slept like a babe on a cobblestone street that winds its way through a tunnel.

But me? According to B.W., I snore in fits and starts. As she's ready to doze off, I deliver myself of a snort that sounds like a 10-year-old boar pig that's just been slapped on the butt with a 2 x 4. And then I'm silent until B.W. settles back into the arms of Morpheus, at which time I snort again.

When that happens B.W. takes to our spare bedroom or goes downstairs and crawls into a sleeping bag on the TV room sofa.

Last month found B.W. and me vacationing in New York City. When I go to the big town, I normally stay at the very inexpensive Iroquois, as I've mentioned recently on these pages. But I wanted B.W. to have a special weekend, so we booked into the Algonquin, her favorite hotel.

On the first night, we ate a lovely Italian meal at Cent Anni right off Washington Square and retired to our small but elegant room at the Algonquin, so small in fact that the bed was pushed to the wall on B.W.'s side to make room for a pathway to the toilet.

Full of pasta, I fall asleep immediately. Soon, I begin to perform my boar-pig-slapped-on-the-butt-with-a-2-x-4 act. B.W. gives up and tries to get as far from me as she can. She finds a spare comforter in the closet, fashions it into a nest on the floor and falls asleep on it. Now the fun begins.

At 3 a.m. I awaken to hear the call of nature (those darned high blood pressure pills). So I slide out of bed and make my way in the dark toward the toilet. Almost immediately, I feel something soft and fleshy under my right foot and then I hear a scream. I realize the soft and fleshy thing under that foot is B.W.'s nose, which is so beautiful it's worth saving. So I jump aside, twist my ankle in the process, then careen into a very heavy chest of drawers.

So for three days, I gingerly get in and out of taxis and theater seats with two ribs snapped off at right elbow level. Next time, we'll stay at the Iroquois. If I crash into a chest there, that chest will collapse, instead of my rib cage, because I think the furniture there is made of cardboard.

B.W.'s nose, I'm happy to report, is as long and beautiful as ever.

~

# Chapter 6

# Going Home Again

*Though he be a fool, yet he keeps much company,
and will tell all he sees or hears, so a man may
understand what the common talk of the town is.*
                                                    *—Samuel Pepys*

MOST WRITERS go to the great capitals of the world — London, Paris, Rome, Tokyo, New York — to gain a sense of the history of civilization. I'm no different. That's why I often travel to Whitehall, population 1,600.

It's a pleasant little town, founded in 1874 by Yankees from the East when the Green Bay & Western R.R. laid tracks from Green Bay to Winona. There aren't many Yankees left, unless you count my old man and Clint Dissmore, whose great grandad came to town as its first Baptist preacher. These days most folks have relatives in Norway and Poland.

I've always been impressed with London because almost anyone you talk to can tell you the history of every nook and cranny in that vasty metropolis. The same is true in Whitehall. Its old-timers can tell you what family lived in what house back in the '20s and before. Bring up one of town's famous sons who went off and made a name, and oldtimers will recount in chilling detail every misstep that snooty deserter made as a kid, right down to toilet training and other gory details.

What follows are some columns about the town gleaned from observation, conversation — even serious research — that I have pursued over the years. can recount in chilling detail every misstep those snooty deserters made, from toilet training on through high school graduation — or lack of it.

What follows are some columns that resulted from observation, informal conversation and from serious research that I have pursued over the years.

# Martin the Mute

QUEER SORT of fellow, Martin. Along about mid-April, we kids would see him toiling at odd jobs along Scranton Street. Taking down storms and putting up screens for widows like Mrs. Larson. Or maybe spading a garden for some merchant too busy to do it himself. In fall and winter Martin split wood, shoveled sidewalks, ran errands.

Martin was of middle age and medium stature, stocky, not unhandsome. He dressed in dark clothes if memory serves, and his overalls were never faded, probably because he seldom washed them. He had a swarthy look about him and he always wore a half-grin, as if he knew a secret but wasn't telling.

As he hacked at a widow's wood pile, or hoed at a granny's garden, we lobbed snowballs or clods of dirt at him, whatever was handy. He'd look up, the half-smile gone. And then one of the bolder kids would holler, "What's wrong, Martin? Cat got your tongue?"

The last was a rhetorical question because we all knew that if a cat didn't have it, a more mysterious beast within him did. For Martin, queer sort of fellow, never spoke and hadn't since we kids were old enough to ragtag around the neighborhood.

Martin communicated with an ever-present Rainbow tablet that he carried in the bib pocket of his overalls. When he finished with the widow Larson's wood pile, he'd appear on her back porch with a little pink sheet that said "$1.50." At noon, he'd appear at the City Cafe and give Ruby the waitress a green sheet that said "Meat loaf sandwich and coffee black." And after a sultry day behind his purring steel-wheeled lawnmower he'd appear at Bitter's tavern with a yellow slip asking for a nickel glass of beer.

Although he was mute, Martin's ears were attuned perfectly to the music of commerce. Whenever anyone asked him if he was free to sharpen a saw or to squeegee a storefront window, Martin whipped out the Rainbow pad and wrote yes quick as a flash and told them when he'd show up for the task.

One day I asked Grandpa Wood why Martin never spoke. And this is what Grandpa told me: "Martin was what you might call a sensitive kid. He had an older brother — he's been long gone — and Martin looked up to him the way younger brothers sometimes do. They were ambitious kids and one winter day they were splitting wood for some widow and got in an argument. The older brother got a bellyful of Martin's sass and told the kid to *shut up!*

"Well, Martin took him at his word and he hasn't talked in the last 35, 40 years. He's a queer one, Martin."

"Grandpa, after all those years, do ya s'pose Martin has forgot how to talk? S'pose he'd like to talk now, but just can't?"

"No, he can still talk, that's certain. A few years back, Martin liked his beer every Sunday. Whitehall being dry on Sundays, Martin would hitch-hike to Independence where they served it, even on Sunday. Fellow who picked him up in a Ford V-8 told the story afterward. Seems they were cutting along at a pretty good clip by the time they hit the County Asylum curve. Darned if the car didn't roll over twice and throw Martin and the fellow out into a clover field. The fellow told about how Martin picked himself up, brushed himself off, looked himself over and said to the fellow so you could barely hear it. . . ." "He *said* to the fellow, Grandpa?"

"Yup. He said, 'Not a scratch!' And that's all anyone ever heard him say since he was a boy."

After I told Martin's story to my buddies, not many of us threw snowballs and clods of dirt at Martin, especially not the kids with older brothers.

~

# Old Rob Bean

**O**LD ROB BEAN strode into my ma's diner every morning, hung his ear-flapped cap on a hook, elbowed his frame onto a stool near one of the sugar bowls, cracked his huge knuckles and prepared for his morning repast.

His Army surplus overcoat was redolent with kerosene fumes and other odors one dared not contemplate. Most folks simply slid their rear ends a few stools away from the heady aroma and resumed sucking their coffee through sugar lumps as they waited for Cora the waitress to bring them their grub.

But not me. I had orders from Ma to stay put, even if Old Rob Bean plunked down at the next stool. For he was a son of pioneers and deserved respect. "You just eat your breakfast and go on to school. He won't bite."

No, Old Rob Bean never bit, but he snapped a lot, sort of like a hungry dog, whenever Cora reluctantly came to take his order.

"A cup of hot water," Rob would snap, "and a fried cake. Are they fresh?"

Old Rob Bean's culinary vistas were as limited as his budget. Breakfast was always the same. A cup of hot water for nothing and a fried cake, or sinker, for a nickel.

He'd stroke the white stubble on his hollow face, muttering to himself, as Cora raced to fill the order, figuring the sooner Rob was fed, the sooner he'd be gone.

Rob took a mighty slurp of the hot water, then grabbed the cream pitcher with one liver-spotted hand, the sugar bowl with the other, and filled the cup back up again. He'd stir it slowly with his spoon until the sugar dissolved, the sip it thoughtfully, a satisfying concoction. His muttering trailed off to nothing as he got down to business with one of Ma's crisp sinkers. First, he'd pour a hefty mound of sugar on his plate, then he'd tear off a bit of sinker and roll it round and round in the sugar until no more of it would stick. He'd pop it into his toothless mouth and gum it around, until there was nothing left to gum and start all over again.

When the sinker had sunk into his slender frame, he'd fill up his cup again with cream and sugar, stir slowly — and gulp it down in a flash.

He'd snap at a willing Cora for his guest check, slide a nickel across the counter, muttering something about "prices these days." He'd rise, button up his coat of many odors, pull the cap down over his elephant ears, stride out the door onto Main Street, and walk, ramrod straight, down the middle of it, muttering at the Chevys and Fords that swerved to avoid him.

He'd be back at noon to snap at Cora for a half a meatloaf sandwich and more hot water, sugar and cream, 10 cents. When the ketchup bottle nearest him was empty, he'd chase the remaining bread crumbs around his plate with an index finger, cornering them, pressing down on the little buggers and popping them into his mouth. And then it was back out into the middle of Main Street.

For supper, Old Rob Bean usually managed to position himself next to Miss Charlotte Ryan, the high school typing teacher, whose eyes would roll behind her trifocals as he stirred up a batch of tomato ketchup soup in his coffee cup and ordered the day's second sinker.

"Are they fresh?" he'd snap at Eileen, the evening waitress, a young woman who always snapped back if Ma wasn't around.

When he smeared it with French's mustard, Miss Ryan's blue hair could be seen to curl around her rhinestoned earlobes.

I always felt sorry for Old Rob Bean, who took off, ramrod straight, for the Big Diner in the Sky years ago. I wonder if he isn't up there right now, looking down at the federal cheese give-away, wishing he were back to take advantage of the bonanza.

~

## Painless Loyle Raymond

JUST TWO HOURS AGO, I was lying on my back in a spotless room, staring at the ceiling. Pinned to that ceiling was a sign that said "Blessed are they who engage in lively debates with the helplessly mute, for they shall be called dentists."

There I lay, breathing deeply of laughing gas, listening to soothing music on the earphones provided for patients these days. Dr. Loyle S. Raymond and his assistant Linda Fiedler busied themselves above me.

I was having a crown installed in my aged head. If you've never had that done, sit down, grasp the arms on your chair and

I'll tell you how it works. There's no way to fix a cracked front tooth. So Dr. Raymond will grind away at the tooth, leaving just a little peg, to which he'll glue a fake tooth that will last forever. Sound like fun? It doesn't? But wait!

Dr. Loyle S. Raymond is so painless that even the Novocain needle doesn't hurt. I compliment him on his finesse through my gas mask and he says thanks. He starts grinding with a high-speed water drill, but the soft rock music sort of muffles the whine of God-knows-what awesome machine he's got in my mouth.

Dentistry was not always thus. As Raymond and the beauteous Ms. Fiedler perform their ministrations and as the laughing gas puts me in a state of mind similar to those who frequent opium dens, my thoughts drift back to Old Doc, the first dentist I ever went to.

Old Doc had been my mother's childhood dentist and she recalled how he would fill her tooth, tell her she'd been a good girl, then present her a sack of hard candy to share with her four sisters. To add insult to injury, he'd always bill my widowed grandmother not only for the fillings, but also for the sack of candy, which cost grandma a nickel.

But if Old Doc was good enough for my mother, he was good enough for me. Besides, he was the only dentist in town. His latter-day office was a mess, his chair, in which you sat upright, was covered with brittle horsehide. And his spit bowl was encrusted with blood from a regiment of Norwegians who had preceded me. Old Doc approached with a Novocain needle that looked like he'd stolen it from a veterinarian's kit.

"Open up," he said brusquely, then he slowly jammed the blunt-edged instrument through my inner lip up to the base of my skull.

And then before the magic juice started to work, Old Doc started drilling. The bit moved slowly. You knew that because the old black pulleys on the drill traveled about six miles an hour. M-m-m-m, they said. Smoke ascended from my gaping maw as the bit whined against precious enamel.

If the cavity was really big, Old Doc got impatient and went in there with what felt like a cold chisel and a ball-peen hammer and knocked off big chunks at a whack. He'd finish in what seemed like only hours.

By the time I came along, Old Doc had gotten real progressive and stopped handing out rock candy. So he'd just slap me on the butt and tell me to say hi to ma and pa. That would be it, except for six months of anticipatory terror. Then it happened all over again.

127

I'm sort of an old crotch when it comes to new stuff, preferring old movies, old customs, even old TV. But with dentistry, just bring on the laughing gas, bring on the FM music piped into my brain, bring on the painless Novocain and bring on the pretty dental assistants. It's a party!

This morning, before I knew it, an hour and a half had passed, the job was done and, shucks, I had to go back to work. As I left the office, I saw a big poster advertising Dr. Loyle S. Raymond's latest kiddy contest. Kids who come in for their checkups without a cavity are eligible for a drawing on a big stuffed rabbit. That's far cry from Old Doc's rock candy.

I wonder if Young Doc Raymond charges a nickel to parents of the winner.

~

## *Haug and Hog*

**HERE IN MY** home town there's lots of ominous talk about a depression. The Farmers' Store on Main Street closed its doors a few months ago after providing the community with groceries, hardware and dry goods ever since Dan Camp opened up for business in 1874. Jobs aren't easy to find since the packing plant closed four years ago. And farmers in the cafes sound the familiar cry of imminent catastrophe.

Pa is retired now and doesn't seem too concerned. But he remembers the Great Depression, when I was but a twinkle in his eye.

The other day he told me a story about when he was 22, a story from a hoard he has packed away in his wonderful memory.

Seems Pa went off to college after high school, but soon returned into the Depression's depths.

"There wasn't much work, but I stayed at home with your grandma and grandpa. I worked at what I could, made wood on Grandpa's woodlot and waited for your mother to return from nurse's training in Chicago, so we could marry. And then I went to work for Palmer Haug.

"Palmer, we called him Punk, was an old buddy who was just married and was farming the home place. Punk told me he was ashamed at what he could offer. Thirty bucks a month in summer. I wanted $35. So we compromised. Punk agreed to pay me for $32.50 a month in summer, $10 in winter, with good food and a roof over my head. His wife, Selma, was a wonderful cook."

Pa and Punk hit it off pretty well, but after nine months, in 1932, he married my mother and found a job as a butter-maker in the creamery.

"That paid $35 a month. It was less than you got working for WPA, but I figured I was learning a trade. Problem was, Punk owed me some money and he just didn't have it to pay. I said forget about it, I had good food and good work. Pay me when you can. Punk felt real bad about that and mentioned it every time I saw him in town.

"Then one day I ran into him and he asked if your mother and me could use some pork, because he and Selma were butchering. I said, sure, and be darned if he didn't show up the next day with a whole hog! And he said now I owe you five bucks less, because that was all a whole hog was worth. We sure couldn't use all that pork, but your mother prepared to put down a bunch of it in cans. The hog was hanging in the woodshed on the weekend your Uncle Floyd came to town. He had a good job at the Gillette tire factory in Eau Claire. He saw the hog and wondered if I'd be willing to sell some.

"So I sold him half the hog and he pulled out his billfold and gave me a five-dollar bill!"

(Not bad, Pa. At that moment you should have given up butter-making and gone into the wholesale meat racket.)

"Anyway, good old Punk still worried about the balance he owed me. When I went farming a few years later, just before you were born, he dropped by and found out I needed a grain drill, a seeder. He had a spare, a real old one. So he hauled that over to our farm and dropped it off. But he was still worried. By that time even I didn't know what was due me. But I said, 'OK, Punk, you're real handy. How about overhauling my Model T?' Punk said, 'You bet,' and he got the old buggy running like a top. And then I told him, for gosh sakes, now we're even-steven. Would you please stop worrying about it?"

The story of Pa, Punk and the pig weathering the Great Depression is not the sort you'll read in high-falutin' history books about the '30s. But it's the kind of story you hear over and over again in my home town.

~

# Once More into the Street

EVERY ONCE IN A WHILE, I try to disprove Thomas Wolfe's axiom that you can't go home again. And once again, I've succeeded. Well, almost.

Last week, I returned to Whitehall. My reasons for going were twofold. First, I wanted to see my parents because I had missed their wedding anniversary and my stepmother's birthday all in the same summer. And second, to offer good wishes and many happy returns to old and wondrous neighbors Henry and Sarah Sylla, who were celebrating their 60th wedding anniversary.

I arrived on Friday evening, had dinner with my parents, then went down to the golf course club house to see what I could see, meet whom I could meet. Not much happening there. Maybe Thomas Wolfe was right. Shucks.

So I headed out, walking down the quiet sidewalk on Scranton Street, wondering what fortune would bring. The evening was hushed, the stars weren't out, but streetlights on each corner reminded me I was on earth. Heat rose from the sandy earth that supported well-tended lawns. I remembered those nights from childhood, on the week before school started, when Bergie and Worm and Gobbles and I walked the streets, wondering what sixth, seventh and eighth grade might bring.

Out of the darkness appeared four boys, just ahead of me. They cut across what used to be Mrs. Smith's lawn, they walked right out onto the asphalt of Scranton Street, they took a left and headed for the bright lights of Main Street, with me just behind them, the old and decrepit fellow who long ago sought the safety of pedestrian walkways.

They were tall, slender kids, taller than we were at their age. The effects of a post-Depression diet, I figured. They wore T-shirts, jeans, just as we had, but they padded effortlessly down the asphalt in Adidas that didn't look much like the high-topped tennies in vogue back in 1948. And their hair was longer, but white, like mine before I lost it. They scruffled along, elbowing each other in the ribs, chattering quietly. An occasional laugh would erupt for a second and then smother in the warm, dark silence.

A sight like this gets an old guy thinking. Like where had those kids been? Had they been down in the rough off No. 1 fairway smoking cigarettes? Had they stolen those cigarettes from the tallest kid's father? Had they huffed and puffed and coughed and choked and thought they were Really Cool?

Not likely. Kids these days smoke on the main drag with nothing said.

And what were they talking about? Were they finally interested in girls and therefore passing misinformation to each other about the birds and the bees, as they worried about their acne and wondered ahead about looking funny on their first dance floor?

Not likely. Sex education took the mystery out of bird-bee stuff long ago and no one does the waltz anymore. Mothers know what to do about acne these days.

And where were they going? I knew the answer to that. They were going to shuffle down Main Street because the annual festival was on. They'd hang around the Ferris wheel or near the cotton-candy stand, with hands in pockets, waiting for something big to happen, waiting for their lives to begin. I also knew that I'd come home again.

I wanted to run up to them and say, "Hey, guys, your lives have already begun. Enjoy this youth of yours and don't worry about something big to happen, because when it does you'll be waiting for something bigger."

But I didn't, because that would have been cheating.

~

# How Ya Gonna Keep 'Em Down on The Farm after They've Seen Minneapolis?

**H**ERE'S A TRUE STORY from the town where I grew up. Seems there was a family we'll call Holmquist, seeing no one by that name ever lived in my home town. There was Mr. Holmquist, who never said much. There was Mrs. Holmquist, who said quite a bit. And then there was their only son, Quentin.

Quentin was a bright young man and when he graduated from high school his doting mother sent him for a week to the big city of Minneapolis, Minnesota, 130 miles away, so he could see the sights and visit his Aunt Aggie.

While Quentin ambled down Nicollet Avenue, window shopping and staring at the Foshay Tower, the tallest structure between Chicago and Denver at that time, Mrs. Holmquist sat at home and fretted about what the young man might be doing. No one else in town who knew Quentin worried in the slightest, because he was the mildest-mannered, stay-out-of-trouble kid in town. Serious. Nose-to-the-grindstone. Mention burly-cue to him and he'd say, "burly-what?"

But Mrs. Holmquist had never been in Minneapolis, and Quentin had never been out of her sight since he came into the world. So she fretted and fussed and waited for his return on the Greyhound. One day she was hanging up the wash and noticed Mrs. Knutson across the fence, doing the same. "Where have ya been?" asked Mrs. Holmquist. "I haven't seen you for at least two days."

"Oh," said Mrs. Knutson, "I took a shopping trip to Minneapolis."

"Oh," shot back Mrs. Holmquist. "How was Quentin getting along??"

But that was years ago and I hadn't thought of the story until last night when I was reading Minnesota author Jon Hassler's excellent new novel, "A Green Journey."

In it, an aging Agatha McGee and her young friend Janet Meers, who have lived their lives in a small Minnesota town, take their maiden voyage to Ireland. On their first night they stay in a pleasant "bed and breakfast." As they talk to their Irish hosts, the family's brother-in-law, George, who lived for a time in Cincinnati, asks them where they're from.

"Minnesota."

George says that's close to Cincinnati and wonders if they know so-and-so from Cincinnati.

"Well, no . . . "

George persists that they must know him because so-and-so lives right across from Cincinnati's public library.

So it goes.

This morning I'm in my office when a fellow named Ernest Kanning of Minneapolis calls. I'd never met him, but he wants to chat. So we chat and he tells me this story: A few years ago, Kanning was traveling in Scandinavia and made it to Oslo where he had to catch a plane home. He had a fistful of silver with which he planned to pay the cabbie because you can't exchange silver into dollars. He hopped into a cab with his fistful and the cabbie struck up a conversation.

"Where are you from?"

"Minneapolis."

"Is that close to Chicago?"

"Sort of."

"I have a brother in Chicago," said the cabbie.

"So do I," said Ernest Kanning.

"Do you suppose they know each other? My brother's name is Peder. I'll bet they know each other."

Ernest Kanning told the cabbie that he doubted that because Chicago was so big.

Oh, said the cabbie.

Ernest Kanning thought the matter was settled. When they arrived at the airport, the cabby refused Ernest Kanning's money.

"I couldn't accept money," he said, "from the brother of someone who lives in the same town as my brother."

And that was that.

So it goes in this very big small world.

∼

133

## My Brilliant Advertising Career

I'VE WORKED in the area of communications for most of my adult life and even before that — as paper boy, high school yearbook editor, college newspaper editor, English professor and now, in my Golden Years, as a journalist. It has been a good life, with the usual modest triumphs and tragedies.

Today, I want to tell you about my first job in the Communications Industry. The year was 1947, the place was Whitehall.

One summer day, I walked past the Whitehall Times, a venerable weekly founded in the mid-19th century, a newspaper given to Progressive Republican politics, plus a healthy swatch of county board and city hall news, not to mention endlessly long columns of local news in which "Mrs. Knut Fremstad motored to LaCrosse to visit her cousin Selma." The Times also had a bank of presses that turned out church cookbooks, wedding invitations, no-hunting placards and auction bills.

Anyway, I was walking along the sidewalk trying to make a cheap yo-yo come spinning back into my pink little palm when out the door came Scott Nichols, editor, publisher, chief reporter and ad salesman of the Whitehall Times. As usual, he was chewing on an unlit Harvester cigar, half of which he'd eaten since breakfast. Scott Nichols was a Pillar of the Community. So he never expectorated (that meant "spit" to commoner folks).

When he saw me, his generous countenance brightened. He told me he'd lost his auction-bill boy. "How'd you like a job the whole year 'round?" said Nichols. "Every week on Tuesday you come in, I'll give you a bunch of auction bills and some thumb tacks. You run around and pin them up. Do a good job and I'll give you 50 cents a week."

The deal was struck and on the next Tuesday morning Nichols handed me about 10 pounds of pink and blue and yellow auction bills, letting folks know that farmers like Ole Oleson had 12 heifers for sale and a whole machine shed full of like-new horse-drawn machinery, as well as three Briggs & Stratton 1-horsepower engines (one operable). Also a 240-acre farm (11 under tillage).

Also a box of thumbtacks and a shiny four-bit piece.

"Do a good job, now, Davey. And come back next Tuesday."

Thus began my career in communications. I tacked up one on the bulletin board of the City Cafe, Firpo's Cafe, the Snack Shop, seven saloons, the Farmer's Store, Rhode's Furniture Store-Undertaker Emporium and all the light poles on Main St. This was hard work. As I walked down Scranton Street toward the Pontiac garage, I saw Chuckie Pederson and Roger Hanson heading in their swimsuits to the millpond. The Moment of Truth. I looked north and south. All clear.

As I stuffed about 50 auction bills into the storm sewer grate at the corner of Abrams and Scranton, I felt a monumental presence at my back. Publisher-editor-reporter-adman Scott Nichols stood above me, eating his second Harvester of the day: "Don't bother to come back next Tuesday, Davey," he said, then vanished around the corner, an imposing squire of the Fourth Estate.

For years, I felt like trash about that nadir in my career as a communicator. Then two months ago, I read a story in the Star Tribune, where I now toil in my Golden Years. Seems a mail carrier in south Minneapolis was caught red-handed by postal inspectors stuffing a bag of junk mail down a storm sewer. Furthermore, he hadn't been 11 years old for several decades. Somehow I felt better. I just hope the late Scott Nichols read that in the Heavenly Gazette.

~

# Great Uncle Jim's Cuban Adventure

**W**HEN WE WERE KIDS, we always had to march in Whitehall's Memorial Day Parade. We didn't take the cemetery program seriously, making too much noise during the speech, scrambling unceremoniously for the empty cartridges that flew out of the rifles after the honor guard shot into the blue skies of May. We always had a big laugh when some high school kid goofed up playing taps. And when Tracy Rice read the list of war dead, we'd individually chortle and poke each other when a Civil War name came up that belonged to one of our families. Nice kids.

Whitehall still clings to the parade and the cemetery ceremony. Somehow, it means a lot more to me these days. Especially when Willie Johnson gets up and reads the list of war dead. The Civil War list is long and includes my great-grandad Dave Wood. The Spanish-American War list is short. One name: My great uncle Jim Wood. His name used to elicit a chortle and a poke. These days, it jangles my emotions, because I stumbled across Uncle Jim's story in an old chest, when I was writing a history of our family. Photos of him reveal a husky, handsome, strapping young buck with a handlebar mustache and a devilish grin. Jim was 30 when the call to William Randolph Hearst's war came in 1898. He jumped at the chance for adventure and escape from the tedium of milking his father's cows and slopping his hogs.

Four years ago, I discovered a stack of letters tied together with a faded blue ribbon. The letters were from Jim to his parents. The postmark was Camp Poland, Tenn. With an optimism borne of youth, he writes of camp life, the swell new chums he's made, how he misses mother's cooking. But most of all, the early letters reveal a blind passion to teach those corrupt Europeans, those sneaky Spaniards, a lesson they never would forget.

As the months progress, the letters come less frequently and loose their spirit, as Uncle Jim contracted malaria and dysentery, exacerbated by wormy and spoiled food supplied by the Chicago meat-packing profit mongers. (I'd read about all that in college, but it had moved me not. The hands-on history in his letters taught me more about the Spanish-American War than any textbook ever could.)

The last letter in the stack ended at nowhere and my imagination took over. Perhaps Uncle Jim was killed in the charge up San Juan Hill. Or perhaps Uncle Jim whipped the Spaniards, went on to the Philippines and met his manifest destiny in a Manila brothel. That sort of thing. But nothing really spectacular happened to Uncle Jim as he sweltered and suffered and deteriorated in that tent at Camp Poland, far from the cows, hogs and hills of Wisconsin.

No, no. At war's end he was shipped to St. Paul, Minn., on the brink of death and placed in the Fort Snelling hospital. His mother made the long train ride to be at his bedside, to nurse and nurture him. After a week, she sent a letter to her husband: "Dear Dave: Jim is as well as can be expected. Poor boy weighs only 120 pounds. He says if he pulls through, he wants to study to be a nurse. Don't mention that to anybody. Mary"

Jim pulled through. He returned to Whitehall and spent the rest of his life as a farmer and a carpenter who built houses with the precision of a violin maker. And he didn't forget about his mission. He married a nurse in 1900 — Miss Olive Tull, a stylish Chicagoan who had been bethrothed to Jim's wartime doctor who died of a long-forgotten disease in Camp Poland after he gave Jim a message to be delivered to her in Chicago. Uncle Jim died the year before I was born, so I never knew him in the flesh. But on Memorial Day, as I stand in the old cemetery and hear Willie Johnson call his name, I know him in spirit.

~

# Dan Camp, The Renaissance Man

**L**IFE IS GETTING so complex that we've all been forced to become specialists. I have a biologist friend who's an expert in Swimmer's Itch. Another friend, a history teacher, specialized in translating the pictographs on the covers of Sumerian wheat containers. I wrote my doctoral dissertation on the early five-act comedies of Henry Fielding. I know a woman who works at a floral shop. Her job? Cutting the thorns off long-stemmed red roses. Enough said.

When we consider how our lives are spent in little cubicles, it's fun to read of a mercurial gentleman named Dan Camp, who was a generalist par excellence. He came to Whitehall in 1874, the year the town got started. He came to edit the town's new newspaper, the Whitehall Times. He produced that wonderful newspaper single-handedly for several years. At the same time, he served as the town's first depot agent. He also purchased wheat from farmers as a Minneapolis milling company's first representative in Whitehall. At the same time, he operated the town's second general store on a site that's now called the Dan Camp block. And he wrote plays and poems that University of Wisconsin historian Merle Curti compares to the writings of Mark Twain, "saucy . . . spicy . . . racy."

Here's a poetic sample, to be sung to a memorable tune from Gilbert and Sullivan's "H.M.S. Pinafore":

*When I was a lad, I served a term*
*As utility boy for a grocery's firm.*
*I polished the windows and mopped the floor*
*And swatted many flies out the big back door. . . .*
*I sanded the sugar, manipulated the tea*
*'Til we had seven grades instead of three.*
*I diluted the cider with a hand so free*
*That I wonder nothing ever happened to me. . . .*
*I overhauled currants and sorted out flies*
*Though what was the use when making mincemeat pies?*
*A woman in hurry wanted stuff to bleach a hat.*
*I gave her Colman's mustard — she got mad at that. . . .*
*Of course we took in butter, about 60 different makes.*

*Some was good enough to eat, some were just mistakes.*
*Some was strong and husky, some of it was afraid*
*To even hint around by whom it had been made.*

Camp left Whitehall in 1910 and made his way to California, where he spent a long and happy retirement. Not many pioneers could afford such a retirement, but my father had an explanation, which he gave me at Christmas.

"You ever hear the one about Old Man Carpenter? No? Well, Carpenter farmed about three miles south of town, near where your Grandpa Beswick lived. One winter he hauled a load of oats into Whitehall, sold 'em to Dan Camp. Camp paid him 35 cents a bushel, the going price that year. When Carpenter got home, he discovered that he'd lost his pocket watch during the trip."

"Pa, d'you mean to say mean Dan Camp stole old Carpenter's watch?"

"Hold on, hold on. Who's telling this story? Nope, I don't mean to say anything of the kind. The next spring old man Carpenter hitched up his team and drove to town and bought fancy seed oats from Dan Camp. Paid $1.95 a bushel."

"Gee, that's a hefty price. Why so expensive?"

"I said they were seed oats. You know, the kind that have been graded and strained through a sieve and then judged the best by Camp's company. Anyway, when old man Carpenter set out to plant, he dumped the first bushel into his seeder and what do you suppose dropped out the of the seed oat bag.? Old Man Carpenter's watch. Now that's a story."

You bet, Pa. And that's the saga of Dan Camp, generalist, poet, dramatist, editor, depot agent, grain buyer, storekeeper and crook.

~

# My Great-Grandma
# Had A Way With Words

**A**S I WALKED around Lake Nokomis last night, I thought of Great-Grandma Mary Wood, a woman I never knew in person, but have come to know through letters and poems she wrote and in scrapbooks she left behind. I think about Mary often when I walk around the lake because of a lake she wrote about just before her death in White-hall back in 1931.

Mary had a way with words. In one letter, she told her niece about the Parson and Sherwood families leaving Crawford County, Pa., in 1844 for the unknown West. And of what a 6-year-old had to leave behind:

"All the life I had lived at that time had been in the midst of scenes of great beauty, as I thought. Nothing of the commonplace, of hard, dull, dusty days, of the homeliness and disappointments of matter-of-fact life. For me, life was at the spring, and springtime especially was a time of enchantment. . . . gnarly orchards draped in filmy white; roadside nooks and corners; the undergrowth of the woods — a riot of blossoms. Then the scents of blossom-time; the pungent smell of mint that grew in the woodsy soil of the old-fashioned gardens; the penetrating scent of 'gill-over-the-ground' or catfoot around the cool spring where we went daily for water. It was enchantment for me to sit by the church window in summertime on Sunday morning and hear the murmuring sound of the leaves of the poplar trees by the brook a little distance away, the distant tinkling of the bells in meadow pastures beyond."

Nevertheless, she was piled into a horse-drawn wagon heading west with other folks who thought they just might do better, where the land was cheap and the soil was fertile.

Week after week, they ground their dusty way across the belly of America. They passed through old Chicago, long before it became "hog butcher of the world." They crossed the blue-black gentle undulation of northwestern Illinois.

When I think of that 6-year-old girl, sitting beside her father, Lincoln Parsons, and uncle John Sherwood, the schoolteacher, I wonder what hopes and fears resided in her young heart as they approached a land where there were few churches, where there were no old-fashioned gardens.

After six weeks on the trail, the pioneers arrived in Lake Mills, in southeastern Wisconsin, just in time to build a crude log cabin to shelter them from their first bitter Midwestern winter. And they came to the lake that makes my heart leap up whenever I see a similar body of water:

"Rock Lake (near Lake Mills) was a lovely sheet of water. Great white oaks spread their sturdy limbs over the banks and water, and far away where the water was lost to sight could be heard the wild cry of the loons over it. ... After washing was over we often went into the lake to bathe and splash around. Joining hands the company would wade out, breast the waves and have good sport. It was a fine place for fishing also. Mrs. Sherwood made the nets and the men would drive a team with wagon into the lake at night and catch enuf (sic) fish to salt down for several weeks' supply."

I read her recollections over and over. In my mind's eye, I see Mary grow to womanhood, I see her travel once again to a new frontier further west. I see her married, and raising five children, losing two of them to diphtheria in one week. October 1877. I see her grow old on a frontier that no longer is.

I want to know this woman personally. That is impossible. But I got close three years ago, when Ruth and I drove to Lake Mills just to look at Rock Lake, which in our century was lined with recreational vehicles. It was, as Mary wrote, "a lovely sheet of water." And for one brief moment, I thought I saw little Mary Parsons make ripples on that placid surface, breasting the waves, having "good sport."

~

# A Busy Social Season
## on the Frontier

**P**EOPLE DON'T visit the way they used to do. The Wife who is Beautiful and I see friends when we are on the job. But then, as night falls, we all return to our respective homes, where we eat, talk, read, sleep, watch television, listen to music and, when the spirit moves us, quarrel.

Whenever we decide to have company, it's always a Big Deal, with a special meal and a house-cleaning and invitations sent or phoned out weeks before. We know this is perverse and sometimes we talk about how little we see our friends in a social setting and we wonder if we shouldn't just ring them up and say, "Hey, c'mon over *right now,* and chat or play Monopoly, or whatever."

And then we think, gee, maybe we'd be intruding on something. Maybe we'd better not. Maybe our friends are watching some really important television show, like "The Love Boat" or "Too Close for Comfort." So we turn back to ourselves and maybe plan a Big Deal dinner party for one month hence. Whenever we do meet socially with our friends, we talk about how little we see each other and what a shame that is and how sometime we might give them a ring and say "Hey, c'mon over *right now.*" And our friends say that they'd come over if we did and that maybe they'll call us and tell us to do the very same thing. But we never do. And they never do.

It was not ever thus.

When I was a kid, neighbors would drop in at our farm and before you knew it, we kids would be napping with the neighbor kids and the visitors' coats in the spare bedroom and the parents would be playing Whist or some such game on the oil-clothed table in the big kitchen next to the cookstove. No plan, no Big Deal, just good old-fashioned neighborliness, followed by a lunch of dried beef sandwiches, homemade dill pickles, cake, cookies and steaming coffee.

And when no one came to our farm and when the weather was fine, we'd pile into Pa's '33 Pontiac and drive around, looking at other people's cornfields. When the gas-ration stamp on the window reminded Pa that such activity was foolhardy, we'd turn in at Aunt Sue Hanson's and visit under the yellow fly sticker that hung from the kitchen ceiling and every once in awhile dropped one of its dead prey onto Aunt Sue's oil-clothed table. Aunt Sue just flicked it onto the floor with a fly swatter. And Ma worried about polio. When 9 p.m. rolled around, the men began talking about chores coming up in eight hours, so we'd pile into the car, one more spontaneous visit at an end.

The automobile helped us with our visits, there's no doubt about that. But I've been reading my great-grandad Dave Wood's daily diary for the year 1872 and I've discovered that even in those difficult and primitive times, the visit was an important part in the life of Whitehall's pioneers.

Dave and his wife, Mary, lived miles from their closest friends and relatives. That didn't stop them from hitching up the team and going for a visit with brother-in-law Shubal Breed and his wife, or journeying to the Sherwood cousins for an oyster stew dinner, or dropping in on Old Man Ervin, who was poorly and needed some cheering up. The trips weren't always easy because in spring the bridges over the Trempealeau River you managed to cross would likely wash out by the time of your return.

Nevertheless, in 1872, Dave and Mary and their kids visited friends or were visited by friends 68 times, sometimes for periods of a two or three days. When I compare that statistic to the neighborliness of yours truly and the B.W. with our fancy autos and paved streets, we come off as recluses.

So let's all go out and visit someone. *Right now!*

(*Author's note:* Speaking of visiting, I get to New York City with some frequency, but I always bring along a bit of Whitehall.)

~

# Dateline: New York, New York

 **I READ IN THE PAPER** this morning an article by Firth Calhoun, who works for Money magazine. He said it gets tougher and tougher to behave as if you're rich. He pointed out that someone earning $200,000 per year might be able to dude out a family in the essentials — the right address, a sailboat, Rolex watches for mom and dad, mink stoles — but that would take everything the breadwinner earned. And thus the breadwinner wouldn't be rich. The breadwinner would be just like me, only his bread wouldn't be as coarse.

So I've given up on the idea. I'd never be any good at it anyway.

Last week, my Beautiful Wife and I spent a long weekend in New York City. We splurged just a little bit, by staying at the Algonquin Hotel, that famous place on W. 44th that was built at the turn of the century, was populated for years by witty people like Robert Benchley and Dorothy Parker and remains today the haunt of famous literary types, as well as regular folks who admire such people. Regular folks like B.W. and me. So we splurged on a room and hung around the lobby looking for Eudora Welty, the great Southern writer, who happened to be staying there at the time. We never saw her, but we did see actress Ruth Warrick and Norman Lear, the TV producer. Good enough.

We stayed at the Algonquin, but after a glance at the breakfast menu, we ate elsewhere, in several modest little diners and Italian *ristorantes* that come up thick and fast in Gotham. On our first morning, after reading the paper in the elegant lobby, we sneaked out and around the corner to a nondescript little place on 45th. There we got our taste of a not-so-elegant New York. I ordered a bagel and lox, B.W. eggs and sausage. Cheap and very, very good. In the next booth sat a couple about our age, fairly well dressed, eating bacon and eggs.

Then the man started mumbling and suddenly he was up and grabbed our waitress, a young Hispanic, and began screaming at her about where his coffee was, screaming at the hostess, too. The waitress said she'd brought his coffee. The man went wild, called her a liar, flashed an I.D. and demanded to see her migrant-worker permit. She said she didn't have one, didn't need one and started screaming back, saying she hadn't lied, but had made an honest mistake. The man kept screaming, telling her he'd see her back "in Mexico, where she belonged." The hostess escorted the waitress into the kitchen and the man grabbed his wife, who had been looking on calmly. They walked out without paying. The other diners erupted into conversation about the man. I ventured a guess to our new waitress that the man probably did this in a different restaurant every morning, just to get out of paying, pointing out that his wife hardly paid any attention to his behavior.

Nope, said our new waitress. The man comes in frequently.

And what was the I.D. he flashed?

"Oh," she said, "he works for the Internal Revenue Service. It was his IRS card."

A well-dressed young man across from us muttered to his buddy that he hoped that crazy guy never audited him. W.B. and I paid our bill and walked around the corner to sit for a time in the quiet lobby of the Algonquin and to look for evidence of Miss Welty's small-town presence. But I was haunted by the crazy fellow, wondering what went on inside his head and whether he'd have been better off in a quieter town, like Minneapolis maybe.

New York City's a fine place to visit, but I wouldn't want to have breakfast there every morning. (We didn't get our coffee either.)

~

## I Have Reservations About Reservations

WHEN I LEFT you last week, I told you of my recent trip to New York City and how thrilled I always am to arrive in that fabled place and be mistreated.

Let me explain about my new hotel. It's called the Royalton and it's very inexpensive, at least by New York City standards. For $55 per night, the Royalton will put you up in a single that resembles the Beautiful Wife's broom closet. I stay there when I'm in town on company business, because my company isn't partial to its hirelings dropping $135 a night in the more-famous places like the Algonquin, which is just across the street from the Royalton.

Last week, as I approached the Royalton, I noticed all manner of people going in and out of its modest entrance. This was strange because on previous trips, the old hotel was so deserted I presumed I was the only person who ever stayed there. I entered the lobby. People of every shape, size and description were lugging shower curtains, old television sets and mattresses out of the tiny elevators.

I elbowed my way to the desk and said to the woman behind it. "I have a reservation — for Dave Wood."

"Don't tell me about it," said the woman. "I'm an auctioneer."

*"But I have a reservation!"* I wailed.

Out of the back room came an assistant desk clerk. He mumbled to me that management decided a few days ago to remodel and there was no time to contact me to say that I would be out in the cold when I arrived. A fine kettle of fish. I picked up my suitcase and trudged across the street to the Iroquois Hotel, which is adjacent to the posh Algonquin. The lobby was empty. My kind of hotel. I inquired as to a vacancy and the tariff.

"Certainly, sir. We have several vacancies and the price is $55 per single."

I signed in. Two minutes later I was in a room reminiscent of the ones I'd stayed in across the street. There was, however, a difference. The temperature, conservatively estimated, was 104 degrees Fahrenheit. And there was no valve on the old cast iron radiator that bounced and sizzled behind a flowered window curtain. I called the desk and told the clerk that the room was unbearably hot.

"Well, there's one thing you can do, sir."

"What's that?"

"You can turn on the window air conditioner."

So I turned the air conditioner to 12 and beat a retreat to the elegant sitting room-lobby of the Algonquin, figuring I'd wait there for five or six hours until my room cooled off to Mojave-like temperature. Up came David Grinstead, bartender at the hotel's famous Blue Bar and a good friend. I told him I'd been demoted.

"How's that?"

"I had to move from the Royalton to the Iroquois."

"That's no *de*motion," he replied. That's a *pro*motion."

"How so?"

"Don't you know?" he said in that New York way of his. "Back in the '50s, James Dean stayed at the Iroquois — whenever he was in a mood to break the furniture."

Then I asked David to recommend an inexpensive mid-Manhattan steakhouse so that I could sup. He enthusiastically recommended Christo's, a few blocks away. The hamburger steak went for $18.75, the strip sirloin for $25. I opted for the latter. I was getting sophisticated.

~

# Of Slip Mahoney, Satch, Little Louie And, Er, Harold Adams

**B**ACK IN 1940, they called presidential candidate and Hoosier Wendell Wilkie "The barefoot boy from Wall Street," by which they meant he may have been from the Midwest, but he had more influence and money than most of us out here did or do.

Whenever I return from a trip to New York City, I'm usually barefoot because I've had to hock my shoes to pay my hotel bill. But I'm no barefoot boy from Wall Street. Nossiree, bub, not me. I'm a barefoot boy from Main Street, a Hick from the Heartland, a Provincial without Portfolio.

So although New York City never fails to thrill me, excite me, I just sort of creep into Gotham and creep out when my work is done. Last Dec. 7, I boarded a plane for the town that never sleeps and ran smack dab into Minneapolis mystery writer Harold Adams, who was on his way to see his literary agent. Harold Adams grew up in Small Town, U.S.A., and even sets his mystery novels in North Dakota during the Great Depression. In other words, he's my kind of guy.

We landed in Newark and decided to share a cab into mid-Manhattan. That way, we'd only have to pay $17.50 plus tip per person. What a bargain! As the cab made its way through the junkyards and the jungle of asphalt and concrete that is industrial New Jersey, we reminisced about what we were doing on Dec. 7, 1941. I recalled that in Whitehall, the weather was so warm that we sat outside in shirtsleeves to celebrate Uncle Ray's birthday.

Harold lived 50 miles away, near Chippewa Falls. He recalled walking into town to a movie in a light jacket. What movie?

"I just don't remember," said Harold.

"Could it have been the Bowery Boys?"

"Why the Bowery Boys?" asked Harold.

"Look ahead," I said.

Ahead was Manhattan Island, its skyscrapers shimmering in the sunshine and haze of late afternoon. The new ones — like the twin towers of the World Trade Center — I can live without. But the old ones, that's another story. The Empire State Building and that pointy bejewelled nose of the Art Deco Chrysler building stir in me feelings I've felt ever since hunkering down at the Pix Theatre in Whitehall, watching the opening of every Bowery Boys movie. The camera pans along New York Harbor, just before the credits tell you the movie was "Produced by Jan Flippo," remember? And all of a sudden appears the skyline, with buildings 20 times as tall as the tallest corn silo in our county. Underneath those buildings, in the slum, lives the gang. Slip Mahoney, Satch, Whitey, Gabe and old Louis behind the soda fountain.

Way back when, I'm sure both Harold and I realized living in the Bowery was no easy life, but, oh, to be near those magnificent buildings!

Harold looked out the cab window and shook his head at the panorama.

"Did you ever think, Dave, when you were watching the Bowery Boys in that little town that you'd ever get to see this sight up close?" Harold asked.

I told him that it hadn't occurred to me that it was even a remote possibility.

"Same for me," said Harold.

Soon the cab was near our hotels. I told the cabbie to drop me off at the Iroquois on W. 44th and to continue on for three blocks and drop Harold off. The cabbie said that was not the deal, that he couldn't do that for a mere 35 bucks, even though the meter read $17.50.

"Oh, that's OK," said Harold, "I'll walk."

I watched Harold stride down 44th with a bounce in his step. He was wearing a light jacket. Never mind, this was also a mild Dec. 7.

~

# Italy Proves To Be
# Home Away From Home

***Dateline:*** *Northern Italy*

**B**ARRELING ALONG on a train through the north of Italy last week, I looked out the window on a field of yellow grain, gleaming under this country's seemingly endless summer sun. It was a wheat field, but not your ordinary wheat field. This wheat had not been cut by a self-propelled combine, but by an old binder, and carefully fashioned shocks of wheat stood at attention in neat rows up and down the gently rolling plain.

You don't see many shocks in the U.S. these days and the sight stirred in me a memory of 1944, when all farmers in our coulee worried about enough wartime gas to run the tractor that ran the thresher. Pa came home from the threshing meeting at Sunnyside School. He looked excited and a bit troubled.

"Well," he said, "The boys decided we're going to hire Old Man Peterson and his *steam* engine. Not enough ration stamps for gas, I guess. Old Man Peterson will come to our place first, I guess. Probably a good idea, but I sure worry about fire."

Ma worried about feeding the threshers, so she just got out the church recipe book and went about her business.

The next morning Pa said I should pick up all the scrap lumber and old fence posts that were lying around and pile them neatly "right there, for the steamer. One thing about steam rigs, you get a chance to clean up the junk around a farm."

A week later, grizzled Old Man Peterson came tearing into our driveway at about a quarter-mile-per-hour, sitting atop the biggest machine I'd ever seen. A Case steamer of uncertain vintage, it was pulling a big old Advance separator with a 36-inch apron that would carry our grain bundles into its bowels.

Following him in an old Chevy with a water tank on back was his son "T-Bone," who looked hungry. "Poof-poof-poof," said the Case, barely working. Old Man Peterson wheeled it around, dropped off the separator, backed off, poof-poofed around, lined it up, so the long leather belt that connected the engine's power with the separator fit perfectly on the first try, as if he did this every day of his life and not years ago, before he and his machines were replaced by the gasoline engine.

That night Ma and the hired girl kept busy in the kitchen, and Pa just looked at the smokestack and waited for morning when everyone would arrive to thresh our oats. The morning dawned with no sign of rain. I milked my little Guernsey, Pa milked the rest and we waited, silently, to see the old Case get fired up.

By 8 a.m. neighbors were rolling into the driveway with teams and wagons, as T-Bone tore down the lane to pump a full tank of water out of the Trempealeau River. His father paced around the engine, adjusting this and that, rubbing his stubbly chin, not saying much to anyone. He was running this show. The teams drove out into the fields, dropped off the field pitchers. By the time they were back in the barnyard with their first loads piled high on red racks, Old Man Peterson had the Case choo-choo-chooing, hissing. Pa looked at the mesh-covered smokestack again, saw sparks bouncing around inside.

Teamsters lined up on each side of the apron and started laying on the bundles neatly, and the Advance gobbled them up. When high school kid bundle pitchers got up to the apron, they'd try to overload the machine and cause the Case to belch up smoke ring. That got a dirty look from Old Man Peterson. The big belt lazed through its figure-8, oats poured out of the sacker into burlap bags that were loaded onto an old high-wheeled wagon bound for the granary. And a pile of straw sifted down on the ground, as Mr. Knudtson, an expert stacker, waited to crawl onto it and work his masterpiece.

As the strawstack got higher, Mr. Knudtson, with a red bandana around his neck, showed his skill with the pitchfork. Old Man Peterson walked around his rig, officiously squirting oil here and there while T-Bone raced across the fields for more water from the river. Young men pitching in the fields horsed around between wagons and teased each other about girlfriends while their fathers clucked at their teams to speed up as they headed out empty. Pa paced around trying to be useful, but wishing it were over and he could bring his team to Chappell's place tomorrow.

Another drama was going on in the kitchen, where Ma and her helper, Leona Berg, were laboring mightily over the wood cookstove. We were recent arrivals from the city and Ma hadn't cooked for threshers since she was a kid. Ma wanted "to have enough," so she fretted and fussed and paced and poked and stirred until 10 a.m., when it was time to bring the wicker wash baskets full of sandwiches and cookies and cakes and pickles out into the fields, along with the huge bluestone coffee pot designed for occasions like this.

The field pitchers sat in the stubble and gobbled down roast-beef sandwich after roast-beef sandwich. Ma wondered if the coffee was hot enough.

At noon, Old Man Peterson blew his whistle and everyone headed for the porcelain basins on the porch, washed off the sweat and dirt and chaff and filed into the kitchen where the oak table had all six extenders added, sagging in the middle like Tom, Pa's oldest workhorse.

The men who smelled of honest sweat bellied up and started grabbing thick slices of dark-crusted bread. I'm happy to report that Ma and Leona had cooked enough.

The snappy stencil on the brand-new oilcloth purchased earlier that week at Stumpf's Store was obscured by big flowered bowls with pools of melted butter perched atop dented Everests of fluffy mashed potatoes. Bowls of crispy green beans cooked just right. Tender young carrots in satiny cream sauce. Vinegary coleslaw, sharp to the tongue. Spiced crab apples and watermelon and dill and turmeric pickles. Icy pitchers of cream-topped raw milk. Peach preserves from the fruit cellar. Platters of sliced beefsteak tomatoes, fresh as the young field pitchers.

Oh, and there was meat, too. Heavy hens disjointed and roasted in sage and heavy cream skimmed off one of the cans in the milkhouse that morning. Home-canned meatballs that had marinated since winter in Mason jars. Roast pork, brown and overdone, fat glistening around its edges.

The threshers ate silently, with determination, as Ma fiddled with the edge of her apron and wondered if everyone was getting enough to eat. Yeah, just fine, but maybe just one more piece of apple pie and maybe a sour cream cookie and just a little more peach preserves on a bread heel to go with coffee. Yours Truly got a chair at the second setting and stuffed his 8-year-old tummy.

"You got a pretty good appetite, boy," said Clarence O'Rourke, Chappell's hired man.

I had to say something back, so this is what I said: "Yeah. Threshing is the only time I ever get anything decent to eat around here." Nice kid.

~

# Chapter 7

# Donka and Bandy

*O*ver the river and through the wood,
To grandfather's house we'll go....
　　　　　　　　　*—Lydia Maria Child*

HEN I WAS a preschooler, I loved to visit with my grandparents Ralph and Martha Wood, whom I called Donka and Bandy, for want of mature pronunciation skills. As a farm kid, I loved to visit because they lived in a big Victorian house in Whitehall that had running water, a bathtub and everything. More than that, they loved me too, made over me and displayed for me their diverse and strangely compatible natures.

Grandpa was a soft-spoken Yankee whose family had lived on these shores since 1635, a trusting man who got taken to the cleaners by sharp dealers wherever he turned.

Grandma's father, on the other hand, had migrated from Sweden in the mid-19th century. Grandma talked a blue streak, and was never, ever, taken to the cleaners by anyone.

I loved being around them so much that sometimes I wished I could just stay with them and forget about going back to the farm with the Saturday night washtub bath and the kerosene lanterns and all the other rigors of country life.

I got my wish in 1945, but only because my mother died at an early age, leaving my father and me with a need for someone to watch over us. Grandma and Grandfather performed that task admirably for two years, until my father remarried and began to make a new life for us. Now that they're gone, Grandpa in 1963, Grandma in 1971, I remember the years spent at Grandpa's and Grandma's with great fondness and have shared those memories with Grit readers. Grandma comes first because she always came first with her gentle husband.

# Grandma Was Close
# With A Firecracker

SOON THE VOICE of the firecracker, the cherry bomb
and the Roman candle will be heard in our land. It was
ever thus, except in the Wood family. We've had a long
tradition of being the wet fuse at the end of the Fourth of July
firecracker. Every June, when other parents were making trips to
the illicit fireworks dealer down by Winona, Grandpa trotted out
a hoary old tale about how his father, Dave Wood, drove the
family into Whitehall for the 1890 Independence Day celebration, how a young rowdy threw a firecracker under Dave's smart
team of skittish bays, how Dave got out of the buggy and horsewhipped the young man right on Main Street, out in front of
Dan Camp's general store.

My Grandma Wood carried on the wet-fuse tradition.
Grandma had no quarrel with noise, rowdiness or mayhem. She
liked all that stuff. But she objected to firecrackers because they
cost money and her Swedish soul rebelled at the notion of spend-
ing for anything that didn't go in our stomachs, onto our backs
or into the remodeling of the big old house where her father-in-
law's buggy whip still hung in the basement.

Nevertheless, when Grandpa's tale of violence on the frontier was over and he retired to his garden, cousin Billy and I
would wail at Grandma for just one little box of firecrackers to
celebrate, offering to mow the lawn every week until 2000 A.D.
All the other kids on Scranton Street had closets full of exotic
explosives and we'd be left out if Grandma didn't persuade my
dad to hop in the '36 Ford and head for that mysterious place
near Winona where they sold the stuff.

"No, no. You go out and play now. When Fourth comes, I'll
have a Big Treat for you that's even better than firecrackers. You
just wait."

So we straggled out of the house disconsolate, arguing about
who'd play Red Ryder and who'd have to settle for Little Beaver.

We awoke early on the Fourth to the sounds of John Berg's
4-inchers sending Campbell's-soup cans halfway to the moon.
We played with our breakfasts in the kitchen, wondering what
Grandma had in store for us. Possibly some movie film trailers
she'd purloined from the old projection room at City Hall? But
that was last summer, when we lit the slender strips of celluloid
and watched them snap and crackle along the sidewalk.

Breakfast over, Grandma climbed onto a footstool, reached

into the corner cupboard and came down with two nickel boxes of Blue Diamond farmer matches, two pairs of pliers, then led us out onto the back steps. "See, you take the pliers and clip off the white tip of the match. Then you put the tip in the jaws of the pliers and hit it on the steps."

Cousin Bill tried first. Pfft! said the match tip. Then I tried and came up with a little pfft! Grandma told me not to hit the pliers so hard because then I couldn't hear the match explode. Soon we had the routine down pat: Pfft! Pfft! Pfft! And a pile of wooden sticks littered the sidewalk under the grape arbor.

"Don't do them so fast," cautioned Grandma from the summer kitchen, "or they won't last all day."

So we stopped for a while to watch Chuckie Pederson Who Had Everything. He placed a lit 4-incher into a toy truck, then rolled it down the driveway, jumped up and down when truck parts flew all over the place.

"Just like that movie about the Burma Road with Alan Ladd," said cousin Bill, who was literary.

Grandma came out with another Big Treat, "lugtug," she called it, which was the chewy cartilage from a chuck roast of beef. "Just like Wrigley's spearmint," she said cheerily. And then we went back to our matches and another riotous Fourth of July at the Wood residence on Scranton Street.

At least there was no danger of being horsewhipped.

∼

## Wrigley's Redux

WHEN MY GRANDMA Wood got her fist around a nickel, you could hear its buffalo bellow in four counties. She came by that honestly. Her father, Charlie Johnson, came from Sweden on a merchant vessel, jumped ship in New York City and ended up owning a great big farm in Wisconsin. His reputation for pinching pennies grew right along with his bank account until 1917 when he passed on to the Scandinavian Counting House in the Sky. Although he gave his money to his two sons rather than his six daughters, Charlie's legacy lived on in his daughter.

When I came to live with her after my mother died, I was introduced almost immediately to her thrifty ways. One day, I hankered for a peanut butter sandwich and she obliged. She brought out of the cupboard a jar of Skippy's that was last opened when Senator Robert La Follette Sr. passed through town in '24. She peered through her trifocals into the jar and spotted a bottom rim of tan stuff having the consistency of anthracite coal. She added some hot water from the tea kettle and let the jar stand for an hour. Then she shook and scraped and urged and coaxed and stirred until the peanut butter sloshed around on jar's bottom. Then she poured it out on a slice of bread and I had my first sampling of a peanut-butter shake.

Grandma thought stuff like Popsicles and chewing gum were for the likes of the Belmonts and the Rockefellers. But when my whining reached the volume of the turbines at Grand Coulee Dam, she relented and headed for the kitchen.

Chewing gum came first. Out of the cupboard came a slab of canning paraffin and a package of strawberry Kool-Aid. Grandma melted the paraffin in a saucepan, added a few pinches of Kool-Aid and sugar, stirred it around, then poured it out on the oil-clothed table top to harden. As the paraffin turned from clear back to white, she got out her butcher knife and sliced it into irregular "sticks."

She stuck a few "sticks" into my breast pocket and sent me on my way. Out on Berg's driveway, the kids were playing Spud and chewing Wrigley's. I popped in some of Grandma's Special Strawberry Chewing Material. It crumbled in my mouth, of course, but when it got warmed up, it chewed pretty well. Within a millisecond of the moment when the crumbs of wax got pliable, the strawberry flavor was gone. I made a mental note to remind Grandma to make the Kool-Aid dosage heavier in the next batch, therefore doubling my flavor and doubling my fun with double red, double red, paraffin gum.

Meanwhile, back in the kitchen, Grandma had set out to make Popsicles from scratch. She mixed up a watery batch of tepid Kool-Aid. Strawberry, what else? Then she poured that mixture into two ice cube trays and slid them into the old Kelvinator that purred away like an old tabby cat. About the time I'd achieved S-P-U on the Spud game and about the time I'd swallowed a few wads of wax, the ice in the trays had begun to set.

Grandma whisked them out and inserted tiny pine toothpicks into each little cube of pale pink ice, then slid the trays back in the fridge. At 3 p.m., I returned from Berg's driveway, tired and hungry.

"I'm tired and hungry, Grandma, but I don't want a peanut butter sandwich."

"How about," Grandma smiled, "a Popsicle?"

"Jeeze, did you buy Popsicles?"

"Nossir. I did better. I made me some from scratch."

Grandma tugged a tray out of the Kelvinator. She decanted one and handed it to me. I grabbed the tiny little toothpick. I sucked the cube. My teeth got achey, just like with a real popsicle. Then I went out into the hot July sun. My fingers cramped as my icy pop went spinning around on that skinny little toothpick like the governor balls on a Case steam engine.

~

# My Swedish Stage Grandmother

**MY FRIENDS KNOW** that there's nothing I'd rather do than talk religion. And, though they never come and listen, they've heard tell that I have a modest gift for public speaking, which I enjoy exercising whenever the occasion arises. The other day one of these friends came up with an interesting equation: Religion + Public Speaking = Preaching.

"Tell me, Woody," my friend asked, "why are you a baggy-pants journalist who gets no respect and not a starched-collared preacher who has the adoration of a community?"

"Thereby, my friend," replied I, "hangs another interesting tale."

It all began in fourth grade, when I lived with my Grandma and Grandpa. Grandma hadn't had much religious training because her father thought church was all foolishness. For some reason, she wanted me to get right in there on the ground floor. So it was Sunday School every week at the Lutheran Church. I liked that. The stories were unfailingly interesting and the pictures in the books exotic. Then one Friday, Grandma read in the Whitehall Times that Junior Choir at Our Saviour's Lutheran was starting up for the winter season.

"You," said Grandma "will be a member of the Junior Choir."

"If you say so, Grandma," I said, remembering how Miss Hanson had always shushed me in first grade.

And so it was off to Our Saviour's every Saturday morning. I'd walk down Scranton Street, where all the guys were playing touch football, I'd cut across the open-air pickle factory grounds and across lawns to the beautiful old church. Down in the basement, in front of that familiar yellowed map of the Holy Land, we'd sing our hearts out, under the baton of Mrs. Ivers, a won-

159

derful woman who had gone to college and everything. We'd sing scales, we'd sing songs, we'd do exercises. This wasn't so bad after all, belonging to a singing group with standards.

So when winter came, I'd slog through the drifts to church, while Bergie and Worm and Bearpuss headed the other way with a toboggan.

A week before Christmas, Grandma had my choir robe all hemmed, white with a red bow, and I was ready for the evening Christmas concert. We marched down the center aisle, all worried that our personal red candles would set the church on fire, after which there'd be great wailing and lamentation, but we made it to the altar, turned around to face Mrs. Ivers and the congregation. We started off with "Away in the Manger," and I figured it was magnificent. That done, Mrs. Ivers paused for a moment, then approached Yours Truly, standing at front and center. She leaned down and, in the barest whisper, said:

"Davey, don't sing on the next one. Just move your lips."

I got the hint and never sang again, except in the shower. But I continued with Sunday School and five years later I was confirmed. Pastor Birkeland told me he thought I should think about going to the seminary eight years hence, after I'd finished high school and college. I was flattered, but knew in my heart of hearts the suggestion would come to nothing.

Lutheran preachers in those days had to sing the order of service. So for a year or two, I had visions of intensive Hebrew study, homiletics, and, finally, ordination. Then I'd get my first parish. But the first Sunday out, as I sang the order of service, Mrs. Ivers would approach the pulpit and whisper, "Davey, next Sunday just move your lips."

And that's how I came up with my own equation: Religion + Public Speaking + Monotone = Baggy Pants Journalist.

～

# *Always Judge A Gift by Its Cover*

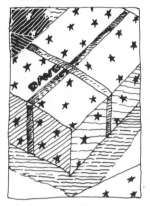

**W**HEN CHRISTMAS EVE rolls around, when my belly's full of oyster stew and I'm near sleep, when I see the nieces and nephews wallowing through billowy heaps of torn wrapping paper, when I see the wives wadding it up and throwing it in the fireplace, when I see what was once part of a forest go up the chimney in smoke, that's when I think of Grandma Wood.

Christmas was a special time for Grandma. That's probably because Christmas was never much in the house where she grew up. Her father was from the Old Country and had had it up to here with the state church, as I mentioned last week.

So Christmas Eve was pretty much like any other night in his household. His eight kids would sit around, wondering what the neighbor kids were doing. Some years, her father must have felt the same way because she recalled the times when he'd stand up, take out his jackknife and ask the kids down into the cellar, where the apple barrel reposed. He'd open it up, unwrap four apples, cut each in half and pass out a half to each. Never mind that the kids could have a whole apple on any day of the year if they had a hankering.

Anyway, Grandma grew to adulthood and she relished Christmas. She'd bake Scandinavian delicacies for weeks — sandbakkels, fattigmand, krumkake, delicate, lacy things — then store them on the chilly porch as the wind blew the dust-dry snow into drifts around the house. When I lived with Grandma and Grandpa in the '40s, they were poor, victims of a cruel economic depression from which they never quite recovered.

So there was never much money for gifts, unless they were usable. A pair of pigskin chopping mitts for Grandpa. Cigarettes for Pa. He'd keep smoking them, whatever Grandma said, so why not, she reasoned, kill two birds with one stone? Wool socks for me. Oh, sure there were some fripperies, too. Like a "True Western" magazine for Grandpa, and maybe a comic or two for me.

The worst present Grandma ever gave me was a bedspread. Even that wasn't too bad because it had "Flying Tiger" fighter planes embroidered all over it.

161

What, you may ask, does this have to do with the nieces and nephews wallowing through billowy heaps of torn wrapping paper?

This is what. Grandma made up for the spartan presents by wrapping them beautifully. Oh, she'd work for days at the dining-room table, making certain that every present could have been presented at the court of St. James. Paper was plentiful and cheap and Grandma, I guess, figured the wrapping was half of the magnificence of Christmas Eve. These presents, before you got into them, were *objets d'art*. She always wrapped everything in several layers of snow-white tissue paper. Then she'd carefully glue on metallic paper stars of various hue, taken from a ton of them she'd got a deal on at the five and dime.

But the best part came when she attached our names. Not with little tags picturing Santa going down a chimney. Nossir. Somewhere, years before, she'd found a bargain on a big box of tiny metallic paper letters of the alphabet. Carefully, she'd spell out our names and paste them to the tissue in green and red and gold. I guess I never saw anything so classy in my whole short life.

Then on Christmas Eve, after oyster stew, we'd gather on the old mohair sofas and easy chairs in the sitting room and we'd unwrap. Carefully, very carefully. When all the thank yous were said, Grandma sprung from her chair and gingerly picked up the discarded paper. The day after Christmas, she took off the stars and letters, got out the ironing board, and pressed the paper for next year.

Merry Christmas, everyone!

(*Author's note:* Now it's Grandpa Ralph Wood's turn to be my inspiration, and we'll start with a Christmas story.)

~

# My Grandfather's Clock

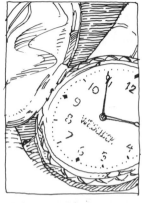

**O**N **FIRST LOOKING** into Nieman-Marcus' Christmas catalog:

What, oh, what, I asked myself, should I buy the Beautiful Wife for Christmas? The catalog sent out by the Texas-based department store must certainly have the answer. Perhaps a croquet set by John Jaques of London? Only $750, and they throw in a packet from the U.S. Cricket Association that includes 1982 rules, the history of cricket and a membership application. Nah, too chintzy.

Oh! Here's just the ticket for B.W. The cabochon ruby and diamond necklace with the splendidly baroque fire-and-ice effect, $135,000. Perhaps a bit splashy with the recession and all. Oh, well, she can toss it in the dresser until happy days are here again. I'll write down the catalog number and send my order tomorrow. . . .

Hmm. . . . What might the B.W. be getting me? If I slip the Neiman-Marcus catalog alongside B.W.'s sewing table, maybe she'll get the hint. . . . Wow! Look at this. "Sleek, streamlined and waterproof. The Concord Mariner watch for men . . . $1,590. . . ."

The picture of the sleek 14-karat gold watch and 14-karat gold fob reminded me of a Christmas present I got almost 40 years ago.

Wind whistled down the wastes of Scranton Street, but my buddies, the Irregulars, met just the same because it was the day after Christmas and everyone wanted to know how everyone else Made Out.

Bergie was happy with his pair of skis, seven-footers, with spring bindings.

The Kid Whose Parents Spoiled Him said, "I got seven-footers too, with spring bindings — and ski boots."

Mick Johnson got a Monopoly set with metal movers.

The Kid Whose Parents Spoiled Him said, "I got Monopoly, too, and Parcheesi and Rook and Chinese Checkers."

Worm Olson gloated over his new basic Erector Set.

The Kid Whose Parents Spoiled Him said, "I got the *big* erector set with an electric motor and flexible coupling and also the biggest tube of Tinker Toys."

Cousin Billy got a Gilbert chemistry set with 24 vials of chemicals.

The Kid Whose Parents Spoiled Him got the 48-vial set. And so on.

"Whadja get, Woodie?" they chorused. I hung back, wiping snot with a crisp woolen sleeve and kicking the hard snow with my four-buckle overshoe.

"Oh, I got lots."

"C'mon, Woodie. Whadja get?"

"Ah. . . I got a bedspread."

"You gotta be kidding!"

"Well, Grandma said I needed one real bad and so that's what I got."

"You gotta be kidding!!"

"It's got P-40 airplanes woven on it. . . , " I said and drifted down the street toward home.

Grandpa came and sat down by me on the mohair couch in the living room. "What's wrong, Davey? Why aren't you out with the kids?"

"Oh, I don't know."

The trace of a tear began to come.

"Didn't you like Christmas?" asked the elderly gent who chewed Piper Heidsieck plug tobacco but never spit.

"It was. . . great."

"Didn't you like your present? That's all we could afford."

My tear trace became a torrent.

"Davey, I've got a little something you might like. Come into the kitchen."

Grandpa put a gnarly paw to the cupboard door, opened it, dug around in a coffee can and came out with a pocket watch. It had a winder an inch long and on its face the size of a pancake there was a word: WESTCLOX.

"It's yours," said Grandpa.

I stuffed it in my pocket and raced out the door to rejoin the Scranton Street Irregulars, a timeless group if ever there was one. It was the very best present I ever got.

~

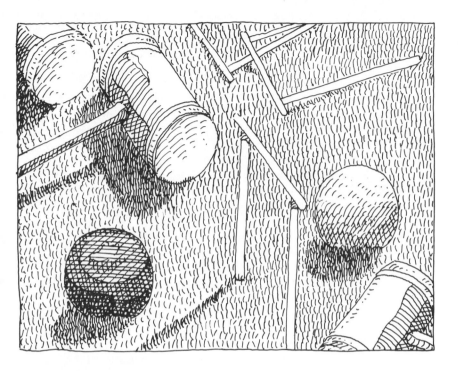

## Click! Click! Click!

**THE OTHER KIDS** on the block snickered whenever Grandpa brought it out and set it up. They snickered and that hurt a lot. So every time he brought it out of the old barn behind the big house and set it up on the flat green lawn alongside the rhubarb patch, I asked him the eternal question.

"Jeeze, Grandpa, can't we ever get a *new* croquet set?"

An eternal answer came back in that hollow old voice of his: "No, if it was good enough for Father, it's good enough for us."

Father was old Dave Wood, a pioneer farmer who died long before I was born. When my pals on the block snickered, I wished mightily that the old croquet set had been buried along with him. They snickered because the paint had worn off the mallets and you couldn't figure out from the deep brown patina on the maple stakes who followed whom. And there was more. The balls were bigger than the balls in the other sets on the block and they were as heavy as cannon balls. They'd been knocked around lots in their day, but even the nicks glistened in an ageless way.

As I whined about a new set from Gilbertson's Hardware,

Grandpa set about in his meticulous way to pace off the official dimensions that he knew by heart from childhood. He set the wickets. Then, with his big boney hands he carefully tied thin strips of old bedsheet to the top of each, so we wouldn't trip over them in the heat of combat and foul the distances.

It was time to play. The kids scoffed and crossed Earle St. to Berg's where there was a glossy new set with stripes on every mallet, stripes on every stake. When all the mallets were gone, the smaller fry, the weaklings, came back to our house and settled for second-best. After a short fight about the order of play, we began and the wondrous *click, click, click* of mallet on ball was heard on Scranton Street and my embarrassment over their age disappeared in a glorious summer Sunday.

The big old balls staggered lazily through the wire wickets and lurched to stops at clumps of grass, the garden water faucet and occasionally the carriage step built by old Dave Wood, for whom they were good enough. Mickey Johnson's hit mine and Mickey drove my ball into Mrs. Gabriel Nelson's asparagus bed. The sun shone down on our innocence, birds chattered in the piss elms that surrounded our lot and the mallets and balls went *click, click, click* until my grandmother went *cluck, cluck, cluck* and called me in for supper.

But not before we carefully put away the equipment. Grandpa saw to that. He looked like a Civil War ordnance sergeant as he packed away the mallets in a huge maple box that reminded one of a mid-sized coffin. Its corners were tongue-and-grooved and, when all was safely inside, Grandpa slid the cover shut with a leather thong inset on the box's east end. It took two kids to grab the leather thongs at each end and muscle it into the barn.

But that was years ago. Subsequently, the sturdy old box and its contents disappeared at an auction of Grandpa's effects. Even before that our family got a flimsy new croquet set with the requisite stripes on the mallet handles and stakes and balls that bounced three inches when they hit the flimsiest grass clump.

As summer descends upon us, I long for that old croquet set that was good enough for old Dave Wood, the pioneer, but not good enough for me. The other day I was reading in his farm diary for 1885, the year my grandpa was in second grade. The entry was for July 3:

"Went to town too (sic) (railroad) station. Pickd up crokay set. Will have sport w/ children tomorrow."

~

166

# Grandpa Held Firm

**M**Y GRANDPA WOOD was a gentle man who never raised his voice or his hand to discipline an offspring. But that didn't mean he didn't inspire respect or even terror in those of us who misbehaved. Somehow, his children's and his grandchildren's awe was in our blood, an inheritance that I think about every time I see some little monster raising Cain, Abel's brother, in a department store.

When I lived at Grandpa's house, he was unfailingly kind, took me fishing and took my part when it needed taking. But one day, he was examining my harmonica and discovered shreds of tobacco stuck in its innards, remnants of a nocturnal experiment of rolling my own behind the woodshed. I returned from the swimming hole below the dam to find him pondering the tobacco shreds.

He quietly asked if I had been smoking.

I quietly told him, "Yes, I've been smoking."

He quietly asked if I recalled that he had forbidden that activity.

I quietly said "Yes, I remember."

Then he said, simply, "I'm sorry, Davey, but I'll have to hold you now."

Hold me? Big deal, Or did that mean he'd squeeze real hard, so that blood would gush out of my cute little nose? I crawled onto his long-legged lap under the oil-clothed kitchen table to find out. He put his bony arms around me gently. And he sat there, breathing softly, the aroma of his sliver of Piper Heidsieck plug wafting over my wispy locks, a reminder that sin was reserved for adulthood.

I was terrified. I began to cry softly, then to beller like a stuck bull. Grandpa sat there, impassively, not saying a word, not telling me the endless stories he usually told of his boyhood on the frontier, stories I loved to hear. I panicked, tried thrashing about, hoping to wear him down. He firmed up his hold a bit, but never squeezed.

Finally, I gave up, letting the hot tears rush down (why did I always cry around this man?), feeling the brass button from his Oshkosh B'Gosh bib overalls gently brushing the nape of my neck.

Grandpa held me for three hours, then let me slide off his striped leg when it was time for supper. He never held me again, never mentioned the incident, even to my father.

Years later, I told my father about the holding I'd received and wondered aloud why I was so terrified. Pa said that was the funny thing about Grandpa Wood. Kids didn't like that sort of gentle discipline.

"I remember once when he held your aunt Helen when we were kids, after Helen misbehaved. (Aunt Helen misbehaved? I can't believe it!)

"Helen was just a little kid and one night she begged to sleep with your Grandma and Grandpa. They said sure. But then Helen was restless, so for amusement, she started pulling hairs out of your Grandpa's nose. First, he thought it was funny, although uncomfortable.

"When he asked her to stop, Helen just kept on with the nostril-hair pulling. He asked several times, then said, 'If you don't stop, I'll have to hold you.'

"Helen didn't think that was such a big thing, so she kept right at it.

"Then he said, 'Now I'll have to hold you.'

"He picked up Helen and took her to the kitchen where he folded his arms gently around her. Helen screamed bloody murder and he just sat there and held. Pretty soon the whole house was up and watching. The hired girl begged him to stop, but he kept on holding and Helen kept on screaming. Grandpa told her to calm down and she could go to bed. But she kept it up, until she was exhausted. When the sun came up, he released Helen and went out to do his chores."

Years later he held Helen's daughter, Nancy, too. Same response. The awe of Grandpa, a gentleman and a gentle man, was in our blood. It still is.

～

# Chapter 8

# My Old Man

*I*t's happy for him that his father
was born before him.
　　　　　　　　*—Jonathan Swift*

WHEN MY WELL of story ideas runs dry, when looking out the window of my office doesn't turn up an old
weather story, I don't worry too much. I'll just say to
the B.W., "Isn't it about time we go and visit Mom and Dad?"
And so off we go to Whitehall. Once there and pleasantries ex-
changed over the kitchen table, I shove Harold Wood in the car
and take off for Quinn Risberg's bar on Main Street. Once inside, our elbows firmly planted on the mahogany bar that
Quinn's father, Art, installed when,as my dad says, "beer came
back" in 1933, we order two taps and Harold begins his harass-
ment of Quinn Risberg. Here's a sample:

"Risberg, I finally found a bartender who uses a smaller shot
glass than you do."

"Who's that?"

"Pastor Kelling at Our Saviour's Lutheran. Edna and I took
communion there last night."

After about 15 minutes, my old man is satisfied that he's
had his licks and then we can get down to business, the business
of reminiscence. Harold weaves a tale about as well as anyone I
know. He can talk for a good hour on his year as the town's
iceman, two years after I was born. Threshing with steam rigs
takes even more time. I especially enjoy his recollections of Pro-
hibition and his one semester at college. He's full of stories,
blessed with an unerring memory and a gift of language. I think
when you're finished with this chapter, you'll know why I'm
happy that Harold Wood is my old man.

# Gilkerson's Union Giants

PA GOT GOING on old-time baseball recently and to hear him tell, it wasn't much like watching the Minnesota Twins play under the new plastic bubble, which is about as interesting as watching your parlor rug fade.

"When I was a kid," Pa said, "the Whitehall ball club was one of the best in Trempealeau County. They even played clubs from big towns like Winona and beat 'em. But they were no match for Gilkerson's Union Giants."

"Gilkerson's Union Giants, Pa? I never heard of them."

"Humph. There's lots of things you haven't heard of. Gilkerson's Union Giants were a barn-storming team of Negroes, don't know where they came from. Anyway, they came to Whitehall every year. Barney Hammerstad, he was a local promoter, he'd bring 'em in on a Sunday and everyone came into town to watch the circus. Our boys were sharp, but they were no match for Gilkerson's Union Giants.

(You could tell Pa liked that black ball club by the way its name tripped off his tongue.)

"Every year, once they took a lead, they'd walk out onto the field. Three of 'em. A pitcher by the name of Lou something, a husky left-hander. A catcher. And a first baseman by the name of Pee-Wee. That was it. And it would be zip, zip, zip. Three up, three out. And Lou, he'd pitch from a rocking chair! Darndest thing you ever saw. People ate it up."

"They must have been fine athletes, Pa."

"You bet your boots they were fine. One of 'em, Cap Evans was his name, he'd entertain between innings. He'd stand at home plate, toss up a ball and hit a high fly into deep center field — that was Melby Park, remember. Then he'd run out and catch the ball. And Lou the pitcher. He'd stand in deep center field, fire a ball at home plate and it would come whooshing in a strike every time."

"Pa, I've heard of the Crawfords and some of the other famous black teams. I wonder what happened to Gilkerson's Union Giants."

"What happened was the Depression. They stopped coming in the early '30s when your mother and I got married. We forgot about 'em. Tough times. I was butter-making at the creamery then and your mother always tried to pack extra lunch in my bucket because the creamery was near the railroad tracks and there was usually someone on the bum who'd drop in with a rusty tin can and ask for free buttermilk, which we'd have just dumped in the river anyway. We always obliged and I always gave 'em a sandwich or some cookies along with the milk.

"One day this Negro fellow came in, down at the heels, real shabby. Wondered if I had some buttermilk to spare. I filled up his pail and gave him a slab of butter — that wasn't worth anything, either — and some of your mother's sugar cookies. Real nice fellow. As he was headed out of the office, he asked me if I knew Barney Hammerstad, the promoter. I said sure, but I wondered out loud how he knew Barney. We rarely saw a Negro in Whitehall then, like now. The Negro said, oh, he knew him from when he played with Gilkerson's Union Giants. 'Well, I'll be,' I said. 'What's your name?'

"He said it was Cap Evans. Then he walked out the door and headed for the tracks to hop a train for God-knows-where. Tough times."

Pa stared past my shoulder out into the distance and just by the look on his face I figured he was hearing the crack of the bat and the ball hitting leather, feeling the heat on a sunny summer Sunday in 1928.

~

## Ever Eat Schenectady Cream Cheese On Your Bagel?

WHAT'S IN A NICKNAME? Habit. Convenience. And every once in a while a darned good story about how a person got his informal moniker. Let's start with habit.

A wonderful man named Arvid Erickson moved to my home town in the early 1930s. He was a telegrapher and came to Whitehall to run the Green Bay & Western train station. People started calling him Depot Agent Erickson. It wasn't that there was another Arvid Erickson in 100 miles. People just started calling him Depot Agent Erickson. Never Arvid. When the depot closed down and Arvid Erickson retired, he was still Depot Agent Erickson.

Nicknames take a different turn to convenience in Stoughton, Wis. My good friend Kate Anderson grew up there and tells me that years back the town had two businessmen with the same name. Let's call them Ole Johnson. One Ole Johnson was the fellow who sold and installed furnaces in the little town. The other Ole Johnson was the undertaker. They belonged to the same church, went to the same lodge, probably even played cards together. When it came time for townspeople to talk about one or the other, they simply referred to Hot Ole Johnson and Cold Ole Johnson. Guess which one was which.

Now we come to the story behind a nickname. A few years back, I read in the obituary column of the Whitehall Times that Mervin Engen had died. I asked Pa who *Mervin* Engen might be. "It's *Cleve* Engen," replied Pa.

Cleve Engen! Cleve was the barber who gave me my first haircut and hundreds after that. All anyone ever called that witty man was Cleve.

"Was Cleve his middle name?"

"No," said Pa, "he got that handle at least 50 years ago, right after he graduated from high school. For a present, his father, Ben Engen the carpenter, sent Cleve on weekend trip to Chicago to see the sights."

What a thrill that must have been for a kid from a little town in western Wisconsin! As Pa told the story, I tried to visualize my former barber as an 18-year-old watching the Cubs play at Wrigley Field, taking in a stage play (might Barrymore have been in town?), or just walking down State Street, that great street in that toddling town. Quite an initiation rite for a young man who was to become one of the best conversationalists in our town.

"Anyway," Pa continued, "after his trip to Chicago, Cleve got off the Green Bay & Western — that was before Depot Agent Erickson took over the station — on a Monday night. He went right to the City Cafe and bellied up to the counter, feeling slick as the dickens and real fancy. Art Wright, who ran the cafe in those days, came up to the kid and says, 'What's for you, Mervin? The usual? A meat loaf sandwich?'

" 'Nossir,' says the kid. 'I think I'll have something, er, different.' The guys along the counter leaned closer to hear.

" 'Well, come on. What'll it be?' says Art impatiently.

" 'I'll have a Cleveland sandwich.'

" ' Never heard of such a thing,' says Art.

" 'Huh!' says the kid. 'They serve 'em all over Chicago.'

" 'Yeah,' says Art. 'I suppose. What they got in 'em, candied hummingbird wings?'

" 'No,' says the kid. 'They got eggs, sort of scrambled, with green pepper, onions and ham. . .'

" 'Well, you damned fool,' says Art, who'd been around some. 'That's not a *Cleveland* sandwich, that's a *Denver* sandwich.' "

And so it happened that my barber got himself a nickname that stuck for life. He was lucky they didn't call him Denv.

~

## My Old Man's First Wife

**I READ A PIECE** in the Wall Street Journal last week. Seems that young farmers in western Minnesota were having trouble finding girlfriends and brides. Seems that most of the young girls leave rural Minnesota when they reach their majority for the bright lights of Minneapolis, St. Paul and Chicago. And the ones who stay behind on Main Street, U.S.A., aren't hot about the idea of getting hitched to a farmer.

These girls told the guy from the Journal that farmers have to work too hard and too long every day. If they milk cows, they don't have vacations. If they raise wheat, they're subject to the volatility of the market. One woman said she quit dating a farmer because he was forever taking her to tractor-pulling contests rather than the movies.

I guess I can understand these girls and their fear of the hard row the farmer's wife must hoe. But when I think back on my own mother, a farmer's wife, I figure she'd be ecstatic about what's happened to modern American agricultural domestic science since her day.

She was born in 1911, died in 1945, when I was 9. During the last two years of her life she enjoyed electricity. Before that, it was put the flatiron on the wood cookstove, heat it up, touch it with a careworn finger to see if it was just right, then iron my father's starched shirts.

Even after the arrival of electricity, she didn't know how handy a home freezer was and she still depended on huge blocks of ice from the Trempealeau River to keep food from spoiling in the blistering heat of a Wisconsin summer.

She canned our meat and vegetables and settled for a slop-pail under the sink that featured cold and cold running water. The hot stuff came out of a reservoir in the cookstove in the winter. But not in the summer, during which time she daily thanked the Lord for the kerosene cookstove that kept the kitchen a cool 90 degrees, as its upside-down fuel supply glugged cheerily during threshing time.

My father never even took her to a tractor pull. He didn't have a tractor until just before her death. He liked horse-pulling contests better. Mother wasn't too fond of the family horses, but always managed to drive them to pull the rope that brought the hay fork up into the hayloft.

Milking time is still a burden for dairy farmers up in this country but not the burden it was back then. My parents milked 20 cows, morning and night, by hand. My mother got kicked across the barn into the calf pens as often as any farm woman.

I remember her picking herself up off the floor, cleaning up the pail and sitting down to the nasty little Guernsey that did it to her and start over again. After milking she had to drag the equipment to the house and wash it there, before preparing a breakfast for the family.

I remember once she went on a vacation. Two days. She and my father hopped in the '33 Pontiac and drove hundreds of miles to the State Fair in Milwaukee. It was a very big deal.

Oh, she had her time off, her quiet time. When that happened, she read biographies like Gene Fowler's "Good Night, Sweet Prince," novels like "Gone with the Wind," her favorite book, and "Cosmopolitan" magazine. She wasn't very cosmopolitan, but she could have been, given the chance.

My mother lived a short, difficult life. But she had her rewards. A clean, safe place to raise a family. The smell of violets in the spring, new-mown hay in the summer, burning leaves in the fall, the crisp crunch of clean white snow in the winter.

And the love of a husband who was proud that she thought enough of him to become a farmer's wife. I guess this story is about my mother, isn't it? But it's also about my old man. (1984)

~

# Pa Gets Smart in His Old Age

SAMUEL CLEMENS, I figure, was one of the wisest guys who came down the pike in these United States. He's the fellow who said that he could never get over how smart his father got once the younger Clemens had reached the age of 21 years.

Pay attention now because I'm going to make my bid for getting in on the wisdom sweepstakes:

I can't get over how smart my pa became once I turned 50.

About a month after my 50th birthday last March, I went out to plant my garden, carrying with me advice my father had dispensed years ago. I thought most of it was superstition, but I had always followed his advice from force of habit. I planted my seeds shallower than the packet's recommendation because Pa always told me a plant will expend too much of its energy just getting to the surface if its seed is planted too deep. I planted peas in double rows a few inches apart. Pa never said why he did, but he always told me that's the way you should do it. And so on and so forth.

Well, last spring, I was in a big hurry and only followed the advice that was easy, like the shallow planting and the pea rows four inches apart. But when I got to the cucumber patch, I took a shortcut.

Pa has always had lots of opinions about cucumbers.

"Here's the way I do it, the way your granddad did it and the way you're great-grandad did it as well," he told me when I was one and 20.

He'd dig a fairly deep hole in the ground, then he'd put in a forkful of juicy cow manure. Then he'd cover the manure with

176

dirt, building a flat-topped hill about three inches above the normal surface of the garden.

When he had the number of hills he needed, he'd open his packet of cucumber seeds. Kneeling over the first hill and using his thumb and forefinger, he'd carefully, insert the flat seeds vertically into the moist dirt. When there were eight seeds inserted in a circle, he'd cover with moist dirt and carefully pat it down with the palm of his hand.

"Why not toss them on, Pa? Why plant them on edge like that?" I'd ask.

"Keeps the birds from seeing them," he'd say with confidence.

So for many years, I've been planting my cucumber seeds on edge with good success. Well, this spring was a busy one and when I got to the cucumber patch, I dug the holes and filled them with grass clippings I had heated up in a plastic garbage bag. (For some reason it's really difficult to find juicy cow manure in south Minneapolis.)

I built my flat-topped hills. And then I took a shortcut. I scattered the seeds willy-nilly because it was quicker. Most of them landed horizontally, exposing slightly more surface than if I had inserted them vertically. What difference could that make? Birds seeing seeds under the dirt, indeed!

I carefully sprinkled the hills with water, and the warmest spring in memory overtook us. After two weeks, I started waiting for plants to emerge. No such luck. Three weeks passed and I started digging around in the hills. There wasn't a seed to be found. Perhaps that big rainstorm two weeks ago had washed them away down the gentle slope that is our cucumber patch.

So I replanted, willy-nilly again. Birds seeing seeds, indeed. No rains came for two weeks and I watered each hill gently every other day. After the third week, no cucumber plants pushed their way through the rich soil. And so now we're deep into summer and there's a big black spot of dirt in our otherwise verdant garden.

I'll never get over how smart my pa became once I turned 50.

～

# My Old Man Loses Some Weight

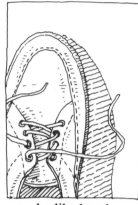

**I**T'S NOT AN EASY thing to lose a leg. But my father is making the best of it.

It happened when the Beautiful Wife and I were vacationing in Italy. Pa has diabetes and he got a bruise on his foot. When we left for Rome, the sore was improving, the prognosis good. But when we returned four weeks later, my sister Kip called to tell us that Pa's leg had been removed below the knee. I put off telephoning him because I didn't know what to say to a guy who liked to dance about as well as any human being on the face of the earth. He also liked to plow for my brother Doug. Besides that he's had more than his share of troubles over the years.

But call I had to, and so I finally screwed up my meager helping of courage and dialed. He answered from his hospital bed.

"Gee, Pa, I'm sorry we couldn't have been home when you, er, had your operation."

"Don't worry about that," said the former Fred Astaire of Whitehall, Wis. "There was nothing else to do and I didn't want to spoil your vacation. And do you want to know the truth, Dave?"

"Oh, ah, sure."

"If the truth were known, I'm glad to be rid of it because it hurt so bad. . . . "

"Ha, ha. That's the way to think about it. Have a positive attitude. Of course, you won't be dancing the Charleston anymore. . . . "

"No, but I'll tell you one thing, kid. I'll be walking by Christmas."

That conversation helped me a lot.

And so when I got my first day off I drove to Wisconsin to have a look for myself. There he lay, in a big white bed, with my stepmother sitting at his side. I told her she looked real good and she said that she'd lost some weight.

"I lost some weight, too," said Pa.

"Gee, you don't look it, Pa."

He looked at me impatiently, then pointed down at the end of the bed, where his foot should have been."

178

"Oh, ha, ha."

"I figure about 16 pounds."

That helped me a lot.

And then it was on to talk about how good the nurses were and how people had visited and how Pastor Kelling dropped by more than he needed to. He told me that Tony Berg, who lost a leg in World War II, came by and told him if he ever wanted to talk about it or know how the artificial limb would work that he was always available. Nothing about his problem, just stuff about kindnesses rendered him.

And then he did his therapy with a vengeance, flirting with the nurse's aide and wondering aloud if waltzing might be a distinct possibility.

That helped me a lot.

When it was time for me to leave, I hemmed and hawed and made some lame conversation and finally I spit it out: "Gee, Pa, I dreaded calling you, then I dreaded coming to see you. But now it's no problem. You've got a great attitude and that'll see you through."

He looked up from behind 75 years of acquired wisdom and he said, "Kid, you've got to be positive. Otherwise no one will come to visit you."

And that helped him a lot.

~

## A Lesson in Oral History

**M**Y FATHER AND I were driving through the hills and dales of western Wisconsin a week or so ago. The black, leafless trees in the farmers' woodlots stood stark against January's blindingly white unsullied country snow.

He sat on the passenger side, sort of hunched up as he does nowadays. At 76, he's still a big man, with powerful hands. We chatted about this and that, what a great heater I have in my new car, we wondered how the cruise control really works and marveled at what modern technology has wrought.

"You know that new high-efficiency furnace we installed in our house, Pa?"

"Yep, how's that working for you?"

"It has cut our fuel bill to less than half. And the heat auditor came and told us if we plugged a few holes in the house and blew in a little more insulation here and there, we could cut that bill by even more. Isn't that amazing?"

He looked out the window at the those black leafless trees whizzing by, sentinels to a past he usually keeps locked up nowadays. Today, I'd be lucky and he would open it.

"Must have been about 50 years ago this winter, just before you were born. Your mother and I were living on her mother's farm, with the breeziest farmhouse in Lincoln Township. When a wind got going, it almost blew the cloth off the table in the dining room. With its old wreck of a furnace in the basement, that house was a bearcat to heat. Boy, oh boy!"

"No high-efficiency furnaces back then, huh, Pa?" asked I.

"That's for sure. That winter I hired two bachelors and my Pa and wee made wood for weeks from Grandma's woodlot five miles from the buildings. Oh, that was a winter colder than a well-digger's knee. Thirty degrees below zero for weeks running. Your grandpa and I would be up at 4 in the morning to milk the cows because the sun set at 4 and we needed to start early to make use of the daylight.

"The two bachelors cut the trees, your grandpa trimmed the branches off with a double-bitted axe and I snaked the logs to the clearing with a team of Belgians. Later, we hauled them by sleigh to the farm for when the sawing crew came up the valley. It was so cold, we couldn't even ride the sleigh out and back from the woodlot. Instead, we trotted alongside just to keep warm.

"Horses didn't like it much either. One noon we'd stopped, built a fire and were heating coffee in syrup pails in the embers and trying to thaw out your mother's sandwiches when I looked around and be darned if the horses hadn't run off into the woods, harness and all. That was some fun, wading in deep snow trying to get them back."

"Those were tough times, Pa."

"No, no, not so tough. I was young and healthy and the hard work kept us warm. And when we got back at night we'd do the chores, then go in for your mother's supper. You should have seen your grandpa and me eat! We ate for 10 men. It was good, simple food. And about 10 minutes after we shoved away from the table, we were ready for bed. About 7 p.m., I'd judge."

As my car shot down the long ribbon of blacktop the state's latter-day woodlots flickered out of focus. Instead I caught two brief glimpses of the big hands folded on the lap of the man who sat next to me in the new car with cruise control.

∼

# My Blood Pressure Rises
## When I Think About My Old Man

**MY FATHER MAKES** my blood pressure shoot right off the charts. He's not a mean guy, pretty amiable as a matter of fact. He's never egged me on to do better than I've done. And for a guy who'll be 75 next February, he's amazingly silent on how hopeless the younger generation is. Nope, Harold Wood is a pretty good guy. What sets my systolic and diastolic numbers humming is not his personality. It's his health.

Let's back up. Five years ago, my doctor told me I had high blood pressure and had to go on the pill. So I take the pill morning and night and everything's just fine. I thought it was just fine until my last trip to Dr. Earl, my sawbones. He took my blood pressure and did the typical doctor stuff. "Hmmm. Hmmm. Hmmm." You know.

And then he turned to me like a wise uncle and said, "You have to do better, Dave. You're on the pill and your blood pressure is 150 over 95."

He went on to say I probably wouldn't keel over in his parking lot, but, still, I had to do better. Like lose some weight, cut down on smoking, and eliminate salt from my diet.

When I was one and 20, I ignored doctors. Same when I was one and 30. But now that I'm eight and 40, I tend to take them more seriously. So I went home and really bore down. After 48 years of salting country ham and dipping my cheese sandwiches in a pile of salt, the way most people treat radishes, I went cold turkey.

I'm here to tell you that a cold turkey sandwich doesn't taste very good without salt, but I've stuck to that. These days, my eggs don't even get salted. I simply pepper them black and swallow them whole. And I went on a 1,000-calorie-per-day diet. Instead of having a juicy half-pound burger at lunch, I went for a walk and then ate a lettuce salad with a gloppy diet dressing that looked like a mixture of Agent Orange and bubble gum.

I pretty much stuck with that diet day in and day out for six weeks. I'd come home from work, grab the Beautiful Wife and we'd go for a four-mile walk. We'd get home and all 130 pounds of her would tie into a triple-decker peanut-butter, bologna and onion sandwich. Sort of an hors d'oeuvre before supper. I tied into half a grapefruit. Oh, sure, I fell off the calorie wagon once in a while, like the time I broke into the freezer at 3 a.m. on Tuesday and ate a box of Girl Scout cookies. But by and large I was very, very good. So the pounds started to drop off and I felt pretty jaunty.

Last week, after six weeks, I returned to Dr. Earl. He wrapped the thingamajig around my arm and pumped it up.

"Thud, thud, thud," said my pudgy little body.

He looked at me quizzically and pumped it up again.

"Thud, thud, thud."

He stopped. And he said, "This is wonderful! Your reading is 122 over 72. We are really getting some place. You can't go off the pill, but if you lost another, ah, 40 pounds, who knows?"

I bounded out of that office like a kid heading out of fourth grade for summer vacation. The next day I telephoned my dad, who drinks a gallon of whole milk every day, eats three dozen eggs a week and dips his sandwiches in rock salt. His idea of medication is an aspirin for bubonic plague. For exercise he watches "As the World Turns."

"How are ya, Pa?"

"Oh, OK, I guess. I've got a lot of aches and pains."

"Gee, that's too bad."

"I had my annual physical yesterday. The doc said I was doing fine."

"How, ah, was your blood pressure?" asked I, ready to pounce.

"OK, I guess — 120 over 70."

Thud, thud, thud, thud-thud-thud, THUD!

~

# Chapter 9

# Better Homes And Gardens

*E**very moving thing that liveth*
*shall be meat for you.*
        *—Genesis, ix, 3*

AFTER I FINISHED my second year as a fledgling columnist for the Whitehall Times, I ran into a dear friend at the Whitehall Country Club. Her name is Irene Everson and she always has my number.

"Your column well must have been dry last week, Dave," said Irene.

How in hell did she know that?

"How in hell do you know that, Irene?" asked I.

"Because you wrote about food. When you don't come up with anything and get desperate, you write about food, don't you?"

She's right. That's what I write about. And why might that be? Because food is my passion. Some men like scarlet women. Others run off to Las Vegas whenever they can or they bet on pit bulls. Still others dress up in garter belts and pink panties when their wives are off serving coffee and cookies at Methodist Ladies Aid.

And me? I cook. I even grow some of what I cook. And then I eat what I've grown and cooked. I don't know why that is. But I do know I began fighting the Battle of the Bulge soon after that U.S. general said "nuts" to the German High Command. Worse, my Beautiful Wife, who has the metabolism of a shrew hounds me continually about my tubbiness. And so what's my payback? A chapter in this book. That's what.

# Spam What Am

**A** FEW WEEKS BACK, Grit readers were introduced to my grandmother's distinctive cuisine. But her story isn't over yet. And it probably never will be because she gave me such things to remember as the Year of the Spam, 1945, that glorious year World War II ended.

The Year of the Spam began when Grandma made her wintry walk home from the hospital after folding bandages for the Boys Over There. She crossed the railroad tracks, paused momentarily, looked down quizzically, then headed for our front porch in a long-gaited dead run. She fussed and fidgeted until darkness fell, then said "Quick, Davey, get your sled. There's a case of Spam that fell off the supply train when it came through this afternoon."

We trudged through the snow toward the tracks, Grandma shushing me all the way, fearful of being caught in the act of depriving a hungry Boy Over There or a hungry Boy On His Way or even a hungry Boy On His Way Back from Over There. But the meat rationing tokens were sadly depleted and now she had a growing boy to feed and one cannot live on bacon grease and Karo syrup alone (See following story).

The huge wooden crate of khaki-colored Span cans had landed askew in a snowdrift at trackside. We lifted it onto my American Flyer and tugged and jerked the laden sled back to the house, then wrestled our "contraband" down into the basement with no help from Grandpa. He wanted nothing to do with our treasonous thievery. Or with the Spam.

But Grandma wore the spatula in the family and Grandpa couldn't avoid three squares a day — in this case, three oblongs. We feasted on Spam 'n' eggs for breakfast. We patted our tummies after a lunch of ground Spam 'n' pickle sandwiches. Dinner? Spam a la saute, with perhaps a dash of mustard. Week in and week out, Grandma dealt us slices of Spam with the deftness of a riverboat card shark. Grandpa got pale and bilious and mumbled things about sinking his dentures into "a darned big solid hunk of meat."

Grandma hung tough. She was raised on a farm and thought eating anything "boughten" or out of a can was elegant indeed. She was the sort of person who prefers a Hostess Ho-Ho to Aunt Doris's very best devil's food cake. Grandma's ability to create gastronomic permutations on the innocent cans of pink stuff was wondrous, and it climaxed — at least I thought it climaxed — when she dipped slices in beaten egg and cracker crumbs, then fried them in butter.

187

After that one, Grandpa retreated to the basement for a pull off a jar of beet wine.

Finally the Spam ran out, as did the threat from the Land of the Rising Sun. We resumed the mastication of solid hunks of meat and Grandpa got some of his bounce back, as we waited for Uncle Mike's return from the Philippines.

Uncle Mike arrived, loaded down with samurai swords, cameras, kimonos, all packed in exotic-smelling wooden boxes. It was Saturday and Grandpa was there with a fruit jar full of beet wine to greet him. But not Grandma. She was too busy in the kitchen preparing the Meal of Meals for Our Returning Hero.

Would it be a beef roast overdone to western Wisconsin perfection? Or perhaps round steak pounded to within an inch of its texture, sprinkled with flour and fried black? (I hoped so.) Or maybe a big fat hen stuffed with sage dressing. Or ham smoked with corncobs? Alas, they were not to be.

What then?

How about Spam, not exactly a Treet?

"I saved three cans against the day you'd get home, Mike," said Grandma. "And look how I doctored 'em up!"

The Spams sat there in a row on the plate, like three little ground pigs. Each was scored like a ham, with cloves inserted at intersections, and glazed to perfection.

Uncle Mike's eyeballs were glazed, too, as he manfully dug into the pink stuff he no doubt had eaten every day since he left the Milwaukee recruiting station in 1942 for Over There.

Grandma and Grandpa left Wisconsin years ago for Up There. Up There, according to John Milton, angels eat just like we do down here. Only their food is more delicate than ours. So Grandma's probably feeding Grandpa Spam, stuffed with truffles or rolled in crushed macadamia nuts. And Grandpa? He probably wishes he had landed Down There, the place where they roast "darned big solid hunks of meat."

∼

# Swedish Guacamole

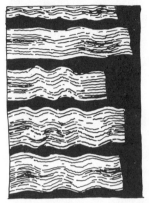

**W**HEN I SNAP off my cross-country skis after an after-work pant up and down the snow-covered ice of Minnehaha Creek in south Minneapolis, I always wonder if my Beautiful Wife, Ruth, will serve me bacon grease for supper. She never does.

But hope springs eternal in the human alimentary canal and I'm certain that some frosty evening, she'll fly in the face of nutritionists and health scientists and famed cholesterol research-er Dr. Ancel Keys and dish up what I really crave. The stuff my Swedish grandma fed me and Grandpa, a Yankee who probably scarfed down a ton of it in his 50-plus years of marriage to the Queen of Cholesterol.

See, Grandma wasn't one to throw things away. And because we ate bacon for breakfast and crisp side pork about seven days a week, there was lots of grease left over. Had she been a wild-eyed anarchist, she might have made explosives with at least part of it. But, no, she was a LaFollette Progressive. Making soap was out because she liked Ivory, which floated. (Probably still does.)

So Grandma had to feed all the grease to Grandpa and me. When the snow fell, she'd bring a big bowl of it off an old table on the chilly screened porch, put it on the table opposite the Monarch wood range, and half of her supper preparations were over. Then she'd slide a tray of homemade bread heels and a pitcher of brown, never white, Karo syrup beside it and say *"Vaer sa god,"* or "help yourself."

Grandpa and I took her at her word. Grandpa, who weighed about 120 pounds dripping wet, would reach out for the bowl, his hand trembling in anticipation. He'd plunge a tablespoon to the bottom of the coagulated grease and come up with his pre-ferred mixture, two-thirds white fat, one-third salty cracklings. He'd place three or four spoonsful in his soup platter and then pass the grease to me.

Then it was Grandma's and my turn, after which we all added syrup, never maple. Grandpa took just a little bit, Grand-ma, a little more, and me, as much as I could get by with.

"Not so *much,* David. That syrup isn't *cheap,* you know,"

admonished Grandma. "And you don't want rotten teeth, do you?" She never mentioned an undercoating on my arteries.

And then we all carefully took our forks and mashed it together, whipping it into a fine froth the consistency of peanut butter. The bread heels were passed. We'd tear off smidgens, dip them in the goop and pop them in our mouths. Smidgen after smidgen, until our platters were wiped cleaner than a starving Armenian's (a mysterious character Grandma referred to whenever I left a morsel of anything on my plate). Grandma didn't have a name for her culinary concoction. But I call it Swedish guacamole.

On particularly cold nights, seconds were in order. If not, it was time for our vitamins. Home-canned tomato sauce seasoned with lemon slices and sugar because Grandma, like many Scandinavians, considered tomatoes a fruit.

My father remembers his first teen-age trip to the big city of Minneapolis: "My friend and I ate dinner at the Nicollet Hotel. It was real elegant, but some darned fool at the table next to us was putting salt and pepper on his sliced tomatoes."

By now, nutritionists and health scientists and perhaps even famed cholesterol researcher Dr. Ancel Keys, if he happens to be reading Grit, probably have worked themselves into a frenzy and are writing hot letters to the editor about this crazy columnist and how parsley salad and fresh fruit and perhaps a sardine or two are the only fit foods for a fit society, etc., etc.

Never mind. I know about cholesterol levels. After all, Grandpa was called to his Maker in the blush of a youthful 84. Grandma reached 86 before she was called to render lard for the Heavenly Hosts. And me? I can't help thinking if I'd kept up with the Swedish guacamole regimen, maybe I wouldn't have this troublesome touch of high blood pressure, maybe bacon grease helped my youthful blood slide easily through the veins and arteries, maybe. . . .

But enough of speculation. It's time for an après ski supper — parsley salad, fresh fruit, and a sardine or two, packed in soy oil, of course.

∿

# Blood Is Thicker Than Sirloin

L
AST NIGHT it snowed. This morning the temperature
dropped to 27 degrees below zero. So I got all bundled up
in my new parka with canvas on the outside just like the
old Mackinaw Pa wore to the barn 40 years ago. I shoveled the
powdery snow, which flew all over the neighborhood as the wind
whipped up, drilling the wind-chill factor to 80 degrees below.

That was fun.

Fun because I was warm inside many layers of clothing. Fun
because the snow was as light as angels' breath, sort of a cosmic
dandruff. Fun because our sidewalk isn't very long. And fun because when it was all over I was going to reward my growling
tummy with a double portion of blood krub. Sounds good, eh?
Blood krub. Some folks spell it blood klub, which doesn't make
it sound any better.

What, a few of you may ask, is blood krub?

Blood krub, pronounced "blut kroob" is Norway's contribu-
tion to the vast array of blood sausages from a thrifty Europe
that never threw any part of the animal away, including the
blood.

Ah, I remember it well. Galumphing my way through the powdery snowdrifts of our front yard, bursting into the steamy kitchen to discover Grandma mixing up krub with her bare hands, pig's blood up to her elbows.

Here's how krub is made: You get a bunch of fresh pig's blood from Sam Galstad, the butcher. You take it home, you mix it with lots of flour, some shortening, salt and pepper, and tiny bits of pork fat. You pour the mixture into long, slender sacks you've sewn out of muslin. You plunge the filled sacks into boiling water and let them simmer until their insides are firm and darkish brown.

Then you fish them out and put them on the cold back porch and wait until it's 27 degrees below zero and you've just finished shoveling.

Then you tear the muslin off the end of one of the long tubes to reveal as much of the blackened blood as you think you can reasonably eat. Then tear off some more. And maybe just a little bit more. Ah, that's it. Then you cut off the krub, seal up the bag and put it back on the porch. Now you melt some butter in a skillet, and as it bubbles you cut thin slivers of the blood krub into it. You fry it in the butter until it gets crispy around the edges. Then you put it on a plate, salt and pepper it and gobble it down.

It sticks, as the saying goes, to your ribs.

Some folks, like my stepmother, add cream to the frying blood krub. Other people, like our farm neighbor, Mrs. Olaus Tappen, season their fried blood with corn syrup. But those methods both are heresies, akin to putting raisins rather than brown sugar on oatmeal. Just fry it in butter and salt and pepper it. That's the true way to eat blood krub.

So, anyway, I finished shoveling the walk and in I went to fry the krub, which we had purchased the previous day at Ingebretsen's Model Market, the greatest Scandinavian butcher shop in Minneapolis, perhaps in the western world.

As the slices of blood sizzled in the butter, growing blacker and blacker, the Wife Who is Beautiful walked by nibbling on a granola bar, peeked into the skillet, said, "Ish! How can you eat that junk?" and beat it into the living room. The B.W. won't have anything to do with blood krub.

What she likes is a recipe her Grandma Schwarz brought over from Bavaria soon after the turn of the century. What you do is you go to the butcher, Himmelfarb by name, you get yourself some fresh pig's blood, you mix it up with a bit of cooked barley. Then you add shreds of lean pork. . .

～

# More Blood and Guts

A FEW YEARS AGO I had a wonderful job. I worked on the road for the Minneapolis Star and Tribune, traveling to small towns to find out what was going on. Not who got elected mayor and unimportant stuff, but what farmers lied about over coffee at the cafe, who caught the biggest carp that spring and whether they were going to plant marigolds or moss roses in the park that summer. Important stuff, the stuff that makes a town interesting. What I was was a minor-league Charles Kuralt without a big van and a television crew.

One of my favorite towns I ever visited was St. Joseph, Minn. It's located in Stearns County, dairy country. It boasts a very fine woman's school — the College of St. Benedict, a convent, a marvelous stone church and 130 years of German Catholic history.

I wrote many stories about "St. Joe" a few years ago, one of them about the St. Joe Meat Market, which is run under the capable and ham-like hands of Junior Pfannenstein, a soft-spoken guy who takes pride in his work.

The market is an interesting operation. Farmers bring livestock for slaughter right to the back door of Junior's place, which fronts on the main drag. The critters are chased, with little fanfare, up a ramp onto a squeaky-clean kill floor. A few minutes later they're in another sparkling room, on their way to becoming steaks, chops, bacon and sausages in Junior's counter up front.

It all makes so much sense you wonder why government authorities haven't stopped them from such outrageous activity on some minor technicality. But they haven't and the folks around St. Joe are the beneficiaries.

I hadn't been back to St. Joe for years until yesterday, a bright spring day with a brisk breeze that whipped around the skirts of the St. Ben's coeds who walked from class to class. My ogling days are over, so I quickly headed for the meat market. I'm 50 years old, remember? (My eating days aren't over.)

As usual, customers were lined up in rows waiting their turn at a meat counter overflowing with the kinds of sausages that always seem to be dangling out of Dagwood Bumstead's sandwiches. Tubby frankfurters, slim wieners all attached, blocky circles of sandwich meat — all of them exuding a pleasant smell of smoke, spices and the fresh meat that goes into them.

I bellied up to the counter and ordered enough to last the Polish army for a week. A two-pound ring liver, its grayness concealing the glory of its taste. A pound of franks. A pound of big bologna, which Junior Pfannenstein doesn't make unless he's got an old bull to throw into the mixture.

"Bologna isn't good," says Junior, "unless it's got a little chew to it. The old bull does that for bologna."

Junior doesn't throw much bull, so I trust him on that pronouncement. And then, and then, my favorite of all.

"Give me two pounds of blood sausage."

"Sliced?"

"You bet."

The 70 miles home to Minneapolis lasted forever. I nibbled, of course, on the big bologna right out of the butcher paper. But it's hard to fry blood sausage in a Dodge Colt.

At home in the kitchen I clanked a frying pan onto the stove, added a hunk of butter. I laid in the slices of black blood and barley and pork. They sizzled and crisped up around the edges. It's always good to be in St. Joe. And it's always good to be back home in front of the kitchen stove with souvenirs.

~

# The Egg and I

I TAKE MY HAT off to the egg.

Only to reveal another one, skeptics might say, judging from your picture.

No, no. I'm serious about the egg and I'm in good company. A few years back, I heard Raymond Loewy, one of the world's greatest industrial designers, discuss his philosophy of design. An interviewer asked him his favorite design in the whole world. Did Loewy mention any of his own, like the revolutionary post-World War II Studebaker? Not on your life. Without batting an eyelash he quickly replied, "the egg."

He went on to rhapsodize about its beauty, its efficient packaging mechanism and all the other stuff that interests designers. And he ended by asking the interviewer a question: "If the egg had been square, how would you like to be a chicken?"

I've been around eggs all my life. I grew up near a little town called Blair, which when I was a kid was called "The Egg Capital of Wisconsin." When we kids visited a friend who lived on a farm, we unfailingly got into the chicken coop, where we stole as many eggs as we could carry. Then we'd throw them at the wall of the barn. Lots of fun.

But what a waste! When I grew into manhood as a starving graduate student in Ohio, I survived on eggs. It was a simple matter to live on a dollar a day when eggs cost 33 cents a dozen. Three for breakfast, three for lunch, three for supper. Scrambled, hard-boiled, fried, in that order. That left me 67 cents to salt away for important activities like riotous living in the fleshpots of Bowling Green.

And three eggs left over for a guest, provided he had a strip or two of bacon to contribute.

Sometimes I tired of the three basic preparations and every four or five semesters, I tried something different. Poached. Shirred. Or raw, with a dash of tabasco borrowed from the landlady. Oh, various egg!

After 10 years of graduate school, I got myself a job. But my love affair with the egg continued and lives on to this day. While my middle-aged colleagues fret about cholesterol, I dive into an egg salad sandwich with relish — and sometimes a pickle or two to boot.

One wonderful thing about the egg is that it's still an inexpensive source of protein. At a dollar a dozen, two eggs over easy cost 17 cents. Add a potato for a nickel and a pat of butter and you've run your supper cost up to a quarter. Have you tried to chow down lately on a quarter's worth of sirloin steak? Or lobster tail?

My mother and father live on a fixed income seven miles from good old Blair, the former "Egg Capital of Wisconsin." Today Blair is into cheese, so don't accuse me of being in the employ of the Egg Council or for having a vested geographic interest in the industry.

Fortunately for my parents, there are still some chickens around. They buy two or three dozen eggs a week from a farmer who lets them (the chickens, not the eggs) run loose. And they've released themselves from the tyranny of the T-bone. Now their biggest worry is finding the wherewithal to buy the natural gas for cooking the little buggers.

But the egg offers even more. Food for thought as well as the tummy. Ponder this question, if you choose. Which came first, the chicken or the egg? I choose not to. But I hope it was the egg. Ever tried to get one of the pearly gems out from under one of those miserable cackling creatures?

~

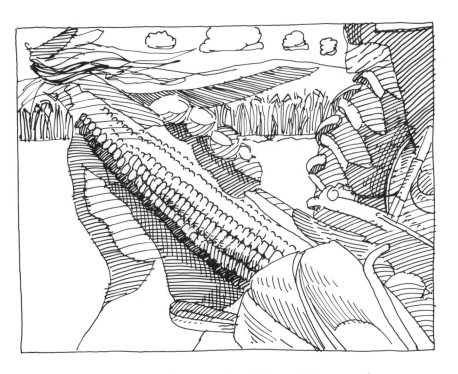

# A Delicacy for The Hog Trough

THE SWEET CORN season is over now, but I'm not shedding any tears. Never cared much for corn on the cob.

*"Never cared much for corn on the cob!?"* shout my friends. That's blasphemous, they say. That's un-American, like leaving your American flag out at night or saying Mom's apple pie gives you a bellyache.

Sorry, friends. I don't like corn on the cob and that's that. And it's not because I can't stand the hulls that get stuck between my teeth, which they do, or because I'm fastidious and don't fancy melted butter running down my forearms, which it does. No, it goes deeper than that.

It goes back to my childhood, when we often supped with my late Uncle Ray in Coon Valley, Wis. Uncle Ray was, and still is, a favorite of mine. Always quick with a joke and great with kids, Ray was the uncle I most liked sitting next to at the table. And when corn on the cob was passed around in summer, I always waited for Ray to give it his special treatment. While everyone else gnawed away like Poland China hogs at the trough, Uncle Ray would gingerly pick a hot cob off the plate, hold it on end to his plate, and take the special paring knife placed beside his fork and neatly slice long rows of kernels off the cob.

Uncle Ray had false teeth.

Then he'd put a big gob of butter on the pile of stuck-together kernels, salt and pepper it, and neatly slide a forkful into his factory-made chewing machine. I'd look at him longingly, he'd smile and pick out another cob and do the same for me. M-m-m-m good! And special. Julia Child, James Beard and Craig Claiborne rolled into one couldn't have created anything better.

And that's the way I still eat my corn, even as ears hang heavy off the stalks in my garden. Uncle Ray is probably doing the same thing up near the Big Truck Garden in the Sky.

That's the way food and I operate. I eat everything on a nostalgia basis. If I liked a certain preparation as a kid, no matter what advances in culinary possibilities take place, that's the way I want it today. You take buttered toast. Grandpa Wood liked to let his toast get cold, before he buttered it with cold butter. Five chunks of the golden stuff. One neat pat in the middle, one on each corner, five chunks in all. Don't cut the slice in half! Eat it in fifths, so there's no confusion about getting some cold butter on every bite.

After 12 years of wedded bliss, the Beautiful Wife has finally learned not to jump the gun and butter me a hot slice that turns limp on contact. As I eat my version, she furtively shoots sidelong glances at me, expecting me to slump over dead, a chunk of Land O' Lakes 92 Score AA butter lodged in my aorta.

Then there's my late mother's shrimp salad. She died in 1945 and Wisconsin farm wives in those days had a devil of a time buying fresh shrimp. So she used the cheap kind, those salty little devils packed in flat cans. And she used miniature macaroni rounds. Her concoction was Larkin Valley's answer to haute cuisine.

Well, nowadays I can go to the neighborhood market and buy giant green shrimp just flown in from the East. I made mother's salad with such stuff just once. Yechh! So I'm back to the flat-canned variety. It tastes like mother's, unless I can't find miniature miniature macaroni rounds, in which case I forget about the entire project, cook up some sweet corn, slice it off the cob and eat it the way Uncle Ray taught me. For the record, I still have some of my own teeth.

Bon Nostalgia Appetit!

~

# The Noble Asparagus

I HAVE A STORY to tell you. It's a heart-rending tale of asparagus culture, patience, and hair-tearing. This story is in three parts and will be made into a TV series starring Richard Chamberlain as me, Suzanne Pleshette as the Beautiful Wife and introducing Charlton Heston as the Asparagus Bed.

***Part the first:*** About three years ago, I wrote on these pages about my four-year struggle with trying to bring to fruition the asparagus bed at the west end of my garden. I told how I'd sprinkled it with rock salt, kept it weed-free and well-tilled, manured it well every year, refrained from cutting one spear of fruit for the first three years. I complained to you folks that nothing was happening, that a puny spear here and there was all I had to show for all that salt, care and manure.

And you folks came to my aid. Never in the history of American journalism has there been such a helpful response. It was better even than the famous old response to "Yes, Virginia, there is a Santa Claus." Hundreds of letters poured into south Minneapolis from all over the country. Some of you told me to sprinkle the bed with rock salt, others told me to keep it weed-free, still others said to manure it well every year and forget cutting even one spear of fruit for the first three years.

And *all of you* told me about your own beds, how yours were so fruitful you had to harvest with haybalers and rent extra freezer space at the local locker plant after you'd fed their fill to all of your neighbors on the south side of Toledo, Ohio.

***Part the second:*** I thanked you in my heart for your good advice and good wishes and wrote to as many of you as my budget — rendered scant by manure and salt purchases — would endure. And then I went out and followed your advice to the letter, then hoped that some of the prayers you offered up for me would be answered at 4833 Elliot Av.

Two years ago, nothing. Not one spear. Zero. But dreams of a flourishing bed that required a Massey-Ferguson baler still clung to my spirit like a swath of alfalfa in an exposed power take-off unit. So I persevered.

Then last spring — 1984 — I was clawing around in the infamous asparagus bed and dug up a root. An asparagus root. It was rotten; it fell apart like Play-Doh in my grubby paws. And then I pulled out another. Rotten. And then, I figured, I had an out. I could give up honorably because of Minnesota's unfavorable, nay, impossible climactic conditions. And so all morning I ripped and tore and dug and swore and dug up every root in that bed I could find. I planted cabbages in their place, by golly, and I knew I'd at least have something to show when fall rolled around. And that, my friends, was that.

**Part the third:** At least I thought that was that. Spring arrived this year — 1985 — sometime in April. And I got out into the garden, digging and smelling the good earth and generally daydreaming about purple eggplants the size of watermelons. At the end of the month, I was scratching around in my former asparagus bed, wondering if beets would be just the thing this year.

What? *What?* There was an asparagus spear sticking out of the gooey earth as thick as my thumb. And another. And yet another. All were sticking out of two dry stalks from last year, roots I had missed in my frenzy to tear everything out and raise some cabbage.

Since then the B.W. and I have had three meals from those two plants. With a little patience I might have been feeding south Minneapolis and renting locker plant space.

~

# Horticultural Economics

THE SNOW is still three feet deep in the garden, but I can dream, can't I? And I don't mean having nightmares about my asparagus patch. I mean about my past successes, like the 14-pound rutabaga Pa and I grew on new breaking — ground that had never been plowed before — back in '71 when the Beautiful Wife and I opened up our Wisconsin hobby farm. Or the bitter little knots that came the year after, not fit to flavor the slop pail underneath the sink in our hobby farm kitchen.

And then there was the great Multiplier Onion Glut of 1975.

200

It all began in 1971 when we moved onto the farm for our first spring and summer and hired neighbor Henry Sylla to plow up a quarter-acre of garden. Henry came on his old Ford tractor with the hydraulic plow bobbing up and down along the gravel driveway. Henry brought a present from his wife, Sara — a small paper bag of onion sets, multiplier onion sets, a type I'd never seen in the city supermarkets.

The sets looked like garlic buds, and Henry, a consummate septuagenarian gardener, said, "You'll like these. They're mild and they'll keep all winter. Just separate them the way you would cloves off a garlic bud. Plant them and they'll come up just the way you see them here."

So that's what the B.W. and I did. Soon a row of green shoots was sprouting out of the red clay garden, a wonderfully productive environment for any member of the onion family. In autumn, we harvested half an empty beer case full of multiplier onions. Henry Sylla was right. They were mild, like shallots that cost lots of the green stuff at a gourmet market a few miles from our winter home in Minneapolis.

The B.W. encouraged using the little buggers, but I counseled caution. "We've just made a start. What if most should spoil by spring? We wouldn't want to eat these things like one of the irresponsible Two Little Pigs. Let's save them for planting next year."

Ever dutiful, ever obedient, the B.W. said OK. Spring rolled around and, true to Henry Sylla's word, none of the multiplier onions had spoiled. So we tore them apart, like cloves off a garlic bud, and planted a new row, eight times as long as the year before. And when autumn came, we harvested eight times as much as we had the year before. That made about four beer cases full. The B.W. drooled over the idea of creamed onions, but again I counseled caution. What if much of this crop should freeze in the basement? Besides, we had plenty of spoilable Bermudas and shouldn't we eat them first? The preservation of my multiplier onions had become A Very Big Passion.

And so it went, until two years later, when our root cellar in Minneapolis sported net bags of multipliers crowding canned string beans off their shelves. Nevertheless, we dragged them to Wisconsin for spring planting. The B.W. finally put her dutiful foot down.

"We must get rid of some of these onions," she said, "or I'll get terminal heartburn from just looking at them."

"Well, maybe so, maybe so," I conceded. "I'll take them into town and sell them to other gardeners who'd like to get a start on these shallot-like marvels that are so mild and well-keeping."

After little success peddling the little buggers, Pa's friend Malcolm Warner finally said, "Sure, I'll take some onions."

I asked him how much he was willing to pay.

*"Pay?"* said Malcolm. "I thought they were for free." Malcolm went home that noon with a beer case full of multipliers so his wife, Marge, could cream them. And I got into the asparagus game.

~

## And The Lowly 'Beggie'

SOME CALL THEM "awful," some call them "Swedes." Some just call them rutabagas. I call them *"wonderful."*

Now that the holiday season is upon us, my thoughts turn to the lowly rutabaga, that golden yellow globe with the purple top that has given me so much pleasure as I've bellied up to the Groaning Thanksgiving and Christmas Boards these many years. Many years ago, Grandpa Emil Johnson, an immigrant from Norway, told me about what it takes to grow an acceptable rutabaga.

"You have to plant them on new breaking if you want a decent 'beggie,'" Grandpa drawled. "And so when Grandma and I were first married, we had new breaking and I scattered seeds over half an acre. Boy-oh-boy, did I get rutabagas, real sweet and real big! I sold 'em in town, we ate 'em every day, we gave 'em to neighbors and still we had a big pile of 'em in the granary.

"Feed was short that winter, so I got this big idea to feed 'em to the cows. So I took the axe and chopped 'em into chunks and scattered them in the manger. The cows ate 'em like nobody's business. The next morning, when I milked, I smelled something funny. I sniffed around and I'll be darned if that smell wasn't coming from the milk pail. Like beggies cooking on the stove. For two days, I had to feed the calves all the milk they could drink and throw the rest."

That milk sounded sort of good to me, because I was raised on the lowly rutabaga. No Thanksgiving meal or Christmas meal is complete at the Wood table unless there's a big bowl of mashed rutabagas steaming between the roast chicken and a platter of potato lefse.

Don't laugh and don't tell me they taste like turnips. Turnips don't have any taste at all alongside that redoubtable peasant vegetable of the stump field. Ten years ago we planted beggies on new breaking at our hobby farm and ome of them weighed 14 pounds and was sweet as sugar; the following winter B.W. and I came the closest we ever have to separate tables, possibly even separate houses. I wanted beggies every night and B.W., well, er, she preferred to ignore them only at Thanksgiving and Christmas.

Here's how we eat rutabagas at the Wood table. We peel them, cut them into small pieces and plunge them into boiling salt water, throwing in a potato if the beggies haven't been raised on new breaking. When they're soft, we drain them, run them through a potato ricer, add a pound or so of butter, some heavy cream, cracked pepper and fresh grated nutmeg. They're ready to eat.

Here's how: Take a sheet of speckled lefse, the thin and floppy potato and flour pancake prized by Norwegians, who bake them on an ungreased grill. Smear on some soft butter, then layer the center with slices of chicken breast, add a thin layer of creamy coleslaw and top with several tablespoons of mashed rutabaga. Then carefully roll the whole mess into what Pa calls a "diploma."

Carefully lift with both hands to mouth. Squeeze out some of the interior into mouth, as if you were eating toothpaste from a tube. Then bite off the empty end of lefse and chew. Continue until the diploma is all gone, then start with another.

Then six hours after dinner, when everything has settled down in your tum-tum, go to the fridge, grab another lefse sheet, smear with soft butter, add a layer of cold sage and bread stuffing, then rutabagas, roll up and eat and watch the late movie. That's what I call living.

~

# Zucchini Victorious

**O**FTEN TIMES, I'm sure readers suspect that I'm just fooling around in this column, trying to fill up space and to get that all-important payment from Grit. I'll deny that to my dying sign-off.

But I've got news today, gentle readers. *Big* news. News that most folks haven't read on this side of the Atlantic. News so important that it's worth the price of several five-year subscriptions to this wonderful newspaper. It's good news, too, not the sort of downbeat stuff about pestilence, famine and flood that you read about in your typical daily newspaper.

Quit embroidering, Wood, and get to the news, you say? OK, I'll get to the news.

*I have discovered a new use for the ubiquitous zucchini.*

Doesn't that have sort of an important ring to it? Sort of like "Today, the Allied forces landed at Normandy," or "Last night, at Ford's Theatre, President Lincoln was shot," or "Yesterday, the first atomic bomb was dropped on the Japanese city of. . . "

No, no I'm not going to tell you that you can fashion toy Indian dugout canoes out of zucchini squash (I told you that last year) or that they can be thrown at stray dogs when they come to leave their messages on your lawn (I'll get to that next year).

Today, I'm going to tell you of a possibility out there in your garden that, for sheer ingenuity, rivals the new chili-stuffed wiener, baked Alaska and corned beef as a poached egg holder.

I discovered the invention while reading a book by Elizabeth Romer called "The Tuscan Year" (Atheneum, $12.95). In it, Englishwoman Romer describes how a northern Italian farm family named Cerotti lives each month. When I got to the part about what Mrs. Cerotti does with zucchini, I almost skipped to October, because I've had it up to my esophagus with zucchini bread, zucchini preserves and the thousand other recipes that a glut of the green stuff has made me heir to.

But I read on and discovered a wonderful recipe that I tried out on the Beautiful Wife, who pronounced it excellent. What you do is short-circuit the appearance of a real squash by picking its yellow blossom and stuffing it.

Out I dashed into the garden, trudged through the overgrown dill, tripped over a burpless cuke vine. The zucchini patch was profuse with beautiful yellow blossoms. I picked eight of the biggest I could find and brought them to the kitchen. And then I made a stuffing close to Mrs. Cerotti's. I ground up six ounces of Mortadella. (Use big pink fine-ground bologna, if you don't have this Italian version, which is wonderful.) I minced a clove of garlic into the Mortadella. I seasoned with cayenne pepper to taste. I bound it with beaten egg and a couple handfuls of bread crumbs. Then I made it into ovals and inserted them into the zucchini flowers and mushed the petals around the mixture. I dipped each flower in flour, then beaten egg, then bread crumbs. And I fried in oil until golden. It was the first zucchini recipe I ever made that didn't taste *green*. It tasted yellow and it was wonderful.

Well now, whaddya think about that? Author Romer warns that Mrs. Cerotti only serves this elegant meal when her husband and the hired men are doing exchange work at some other farm. Just think of the options. Maybe you could make the stuffing out of ground-up zucchini squash that made it past the flower stage. Then you'd really be accomplishing something in the fight against zucchini pollution in America.

Buon, as they say in Italy, appetito!

~

# Toby and The Mushrooms

L AST FALL our good friend Theophile Mares of New
Prague, Minn., called Ruth and me with a bit of news.

"I'm sick of picking wild mushrooms and giving them
to you. From now on, if you want wild mushrooms, you can
come and pick them yourself. I'll show you where they are."

So the next day we drove south from Minneapolis to Theophile's charming little Czech town where everyone calls him
Toby. We got into Toby's car and went to his secret mushroom
woodlot. We picked and picked and picked. Toby picked, too,
and supervised and complained that no one picks mushrooms
anymore and picked some more and supervised and complained
as is his wont.

After an hour we had about 20 pounds of beautiful fall
mushrooms. I asked Toby what they were called and he said he
didn't know, but that there was nothing wrong with them, that
he picked them as a kid 60 years ago and they never hurt him
one bit.

So we took them home and, as per his instructions, we
soaked them in several baths of salt water, then we patted them

dry and sauteed them in a greaseless pan until much of their liquid had evaporated. Then we added butter and garlic and cooked them some more. We ate as much as we could hold, then froze the rest.

No, no. I'm not trying to muscle in on Grit food columnist Carl Larsen. This isn't a recipe column. It's a story and I'm getting to it.

Anyway, the mushrooms reposed in the freezer until it was time for a party we were throwing. What would be more exotic than a wild mushroom loaf to present to our guests? So I thawed a bunch of mushrooms and whipped up a wonderful loaf.

Then I made a big mistake. I read Jon Hassler's new book, "A Green Journey." It's a marvelous book, featuring Hassler's wonderful character Agatha McGee, an elderly Roman Catholic schoolmarm who in this novel goes to Ireland on a trip. In one of the subplots, her American bishop gets hooked up with an Irish priest who insists on feeding him wild mushrooms. As they're dining, the American bishop and the Irish priest notice the priest's dog lying unconscious on the floor after also feasting on the wild mushrooms. I won't give away the punchline, but suffice it to say both bishop and priest make a trip to the hospital to have their stomachs pumped.

And so there sat the mushroom loaf in the fridge, waiting for the guests to arrive. Should I serve it? Or shouldn't I? Ruth and I had eaten lots of the little buggers without incident last fall. But what if there was a poison one we missed? Just one?

Oh, what the heck? If priests and bishops can get their stomachs pumped, why not our guests? Besides, Jon Hassler, the novelist, is a guy who earns a living making up cock-and-bull stories. That sort of thing doesn't happen in real life, does it?

So we served the mushroom loaf and everyone remarked on how delicious it was. I just stood in a corner and waited for people to drop to the floor in a fit. And I wondered what sort of an excuse I could make. Could I blame Theophile "Toby" Mares? Would my insurance cover such events? This was not my favorite party. Under my breath I cursed the day I took up Jon Hassler's most excellent novel.

Then everyone went home and I breathed a sigh of relief. I breathed an even bigger one when all the guests turned up healthy a day later.

~

# Remember Restaurants
# Called Eats?

**M**Y STEPMOTHER worked for half a century in the restaurant business and so when she married my father I had the privilege of eating in one of her restaurants almost every day of my young life.

Hers weren't fancy restaurants with fancy names. One was called The Snack Shop, because a lot of people took a noon snack there. Another was called the City Cafe and had been for as long as any of the old-timers could remember. She owned one other restaurant, but I can't remember the name of it. Probably it was just called "Cafe" or "Eats."

I remember the City Cafe best. It was a classic small-town restaurant, the sort that dominated the American scene for the first 50 years of our century. Walk in between two huge sidewalk windows. On your right was the cigar counter, with a porcelain and chrome soda fountain behind it. On your right was a wall hung with auction bills. A long counter with stools stretched along the north wall. At one end was a Hires root beer barrel, at the other, several gallon jars of cookies. Across the aisles were high wooden booths that had left many generations of behinds numb after half-hour sits. At the back were about 15 tables covered with checkered oilcloth. Overhead, five fans revolved lazily in the summer months.

The food was excellent, made from scratch, and so was the coffee at 10 cents the cup.

I loved that restaurant and right now I can taste my stepmother's hot beef sandwich with mashed potatoes and gravy. Seventy-five cents. Or maybe a chocolate ice cream soda, finished off with a needle-sharp shot of seltzer from the fountain. Thirty cents. It was a simple place and it was plenty good for me.

You don't find restaurants like that these days. These days, we're into ferns and trendy and theme. In half of the restaurants these days, you need a machete knife to cut your way to a table. And the menus vary from year to year: One year it's broccoli quiche, the next it's tofu lasagna. And always alfalfa sprout salads. And don't forget all the cutesy stuff. There's one popular restaurant in Minneapolis that serves its coffee in half-pint Mason jars to which have been attached wooden handles.

But most disturbing is the trend toward theme. I ate in a restaurant in San Jose, Calif., that featured a Western motif. I walked in and looked out over the main dining room to see several covered wagons pulled into a circle. The hostess showed me into a covered wagon, where I sat, alone, and ate a bowl of over-priced chile con carne (it was terrible) and looked out at the fake bonfire that burned in the middle of the circle. As I left that monument to stupidity, I kept looking on the floor so as not to step on a cow pie or a horse apple.

Just this morning, I ate breakfast in our company cafeteria. I thought the cooks and counter people looked strange. I sat down with my egg and toast at 7:30 a.m. and the loudspeakers began blasting out "There's a Whole Lot of Shaking Going On."

Dorinda the checker looked out from under her pony-tailed hair-do and explained that this was "Fifties Week" at the cafeteria during which time diners would be treated to all sorts of 1950s music and the help had to come dressed in '50s costumes. I'm not relishing the prospect of breakfast with rock-and-roll.

What this country needs is just one more type of trendy restaurant. I think it should have a cigar case, a long counter with a Hires root beer barrel. It's specialty? Hot beef sandwiches with mashed potatoes and gravy.

~

# Recipe For A Perfect Fall Sunday Afternoon

There are many just-fine Sunday afternoons, and there are some mediocre ones. Then there are perfect ones, those perfect Sunday afternoons in autumn. The recipe is a simple one.

**INGREDIENTS:**

1 Televised Packers-Vikings Game

1 TV Showing of "The Magnificent Ambersons"

1 TV Showing of Bette Davis in "The Old Maid"

1 Busy Wife who is Beautiful

1 Big Soup Bone

1 Chuck Roast at 89 cents per pound

1 cupboard full of spices and staples

The last of the garden vegetables moldering in the refrigerator

Method of Preparation:

Get home from church. Turn the heat to about 15 degrees Fahrenheit outside, 68 inside. Put on warm pajamas, wooly socks, no slippers. Patter down to the kitchen, turn on the football game, fill up the soup kettle with water and plop in the soup bone, a couple ribs of celery, a clove-studded onion, some peppercorns, a bay leaf and the butt of a rutabaga, then turn on the flame. As you trim the chuck roast and slice onions, carrots, celery and rutabaga, watch the Minnesota Vikings run all over the Packers of Wisconsin, your home state.

Open a bottle of wine and pour yourself a glass.

From time to time walk into the study and tell the Wife who is Beautiful that you're glad to no longer be teaching, because now you're free on Sundays. Don't do this too often, lest you spoil the recipe. (She's grading student papers.)

When the soup bone's flavor has entered the broth, strain out the refuse and put the broth on the porch to cool.

The next step is *very important:* Return to the kitchen to putter and to watch the Green Bay Packers score 21 points in the final quarter to win the game and uphold Wisconsin's honor.

Then call several friends who are Vikings fans and say clever things, like "How about them Packers! How about them Packers!!" Hang up quickly before the telephone cord melts.

Watch the postgame call-in program and chuckle a bit over the exasperation of Minnesotans who call the experts and wonder what happened. By now, the fat has coagulated at the top of the broth on the porch. Gingerly lift it off in a sheet and toss it out onto a snow drift. The birds have to eat, too.

Put the broth back on the burner and add the carefully trimmed and cubed chuck roast. Reduce to a simmer, cover the pot and go into the den and turn to Channel 41. You've missed 18 minutes of "The Magnificent Ambersons," but that doesn't matter because you know the movie by heart.

As the steam from the bubbling pot fogs the windows, listen to Orson Welles' narration, oilier than the fat in the snow drift. Then watch Tim Holt make a fool of himself, marvel at how chubby Anne Baxter was in 1942, feel sorry for Joseph Cotten in his ill-fated quest for the hand of Dolores Costello.

When the Wellesian credits roll at the end, return to the kitchen to find the chuck roast is fork-tender. Pour in a bowl of chopped vegetables. When they're almost done, correct seasoning and whomp up some dumplings made of bread crumbs, parsley, flour, eggs, cream and a grating of fresh nutmeg. Carefully spoon them onto the glistening surface of the just-bubbling soup, turn off the heat and cover. Return to the den and Channel 9's presentation of "The Old Maid" and watch Bette Davis grow old ungracefully.

When the credits roll, invite your B.W. into the study. Give her lots of meat in her soup. She needs to keep up her strength, but don't mention it.

~

# Conclusion

I'd like to linger on this conclusion, tell you how much I enjoyed assembling this collection of columns. But I'll just have to say that's all folks! (I'm facing another deadline.)

# POSTSCRIPT

*The Stupendous Fourth Estate,
    whose wide world-embracing
influences what eye can take in?*
        *—Thomas Carlyle*

*The freedom of the press is one of the
    great bulwarks of liberty, and can never be
restrained but by despotic governments.*
        **—George Mason**

*A free press is not a privilege
    but an organic necessity in a great society.*
        **—Walter Lippmann**

*The press is a sort of wild animal in our
    midst — restless, gigantic, always seeking new ways
to use its strength. . . .*
        **—Zechariah Chafee, Jr.**

HEY, I'M NOT quite finished yet. It's Feb. 28 and we're ready to go to press, to put this book to bed, as they say in the publications industry.

But I'm not ready to go to bed, not when you have quotations like those above to substantiate. No, no, don't worry. I don't have miles to go before I sleep. Just a few pages.

I want to say a few words about the Power of the Press.

I'm not the first to write about the Fourth Estate's power and I probably won't be the last.

No less a man than Thomas Carlyle did. And older readers will remember the power exercised by the Hearst Press and the resultant Spanish American War. Just think of what that meant to the political career of Teddy Roosevelt. And what it meant to my Great Uncle Jim, who went to war and got sicker than a dog.

Movie fans will remember the same William Randolph Hearst who became the unsympathetic centerpiece of Orson Welles classic, "Citizen Kane." Welles, the *wunderkind* of the cinema, who became a fat guy and hawked cheap wine on TV in his later years, got his comeuppance when Hearst used his considerable influence to keep his wonderful movie out of most of the big theatre chains in the U.S. Some power, some press.

Younger readers, the college kids I used to teach, will delight in remembering Woodward and Bernstein and how they found "Deep Throat," then broke open the the Watergate puzzle, which resulted in the political demise of Richard Milhaus Nixon and thereby flooded every journalism school in the country with would be investigative reporter heroes, modeled on Robert Redford and Dustin Hoffman. This depressed reporters' salaries all over the world, alas. Sometimes the power of the press has depressing side effects.

Some of the power is used to further selfish ends. In other cases, crooks get what's coming. On the whole, I'm happy to reside in the United States where freedom of the press is an important part of our life, whatever the salaries. That was brought home in 1970, when the Beautiful Wife and I honeymooned in Spain. We arrived on Saturday. On Sunday morning, I ran out to pick up some bread, some coffee and the Sunday paper. What a disappointment! Back then Francisco Franco was still in power, and Madrid's biggest newspaper was mighty thin, about the size of the Whitehall Times when the editor is taking his annual fishing trip. That's because only one side of the Spanish story was being told; after all, Franco didn't want his countrymen reading about the other side. On that particular day, if memory serves, the entire newspaper was devoted to an obituary of one of Franco's compadres, General Munoz Grandes. I was especially bored by the story recounting all the foreign military honors bestowed on him. Oh, he'd won them from governments like Hitler's and Eisenhower's. Quite a guy. Whew!

But the Power of the Press doesn't only work its wonders on war, political corruption and the tyranny of dictatorship. This fact has been indelibly stamped on my consciousness.

That's because, as a columnist for Grit, I recently whiffed the sweet smell of power, wallowed in waves of self-congratulation for exercising that power.

About a month ago, after thinking I had finished "My

Mother the Arsonist & Other Toasty Tales," I wrote a yet another column for Grit, in which I worried about the imminent decline of a great restaurant, a monument to haut cuisine, a veritable Tour D'Argent of Minneapolis's printing district, The Four Seasons come to the state of Two Seasons. A restaurant at which I dine every day.

You guessed it. The Little Wagon, home of the Squaretable Wits. After the story ran, I knew I wasn't quite finished with this book.

But let's back up a bit. This is what I wrote:

"Forget about the Bengal tiger. Forget about the Great White Whale. Forget about the charging rhinoceros, the rogue elephant, the grizzly bear and the lordly elk.

"In my book, the sardine is the noblest of all earth's creatures.

"It's not the biggest of earth's fauna, nor the strongest, and probably not the most beautiful, although the beauty part is arguable, especially when you slide one of those dead little critters onto a slice of buttered bread and garnish it with a ring of sweet Bermuda onion.

"I was introduced to the Noble Sardine at a tender age. I lived with Grandma and Grandpa in their old rooming house when I was a fourth grader. Back then, Saturday night was *not* the loneliest night of the week at the rooming house, despite what the song said. No, Saturday was the night Grandma peeled open several cans of sardines, plus a box of saltines. Her bachelor roomers would arrive home from work, take their baths and repair to the old kitchen, bringing with them their beverages of choice. And of Grandma and Grandpa's. That was the deal. If the hosts provided the sardines, the roomers brought something with which to wash it down.

"Lyder Nelson, the buttermaker, always brought me a bottle of my favorite, Orange Crush.

"And then there was much chomping and chewing and oohing and aahing. Grandma always bought cheap overgrown sardines, in the big oval cans, the kind that were masked in mustard and tomato sauce, which, if memory serves, cost about 10 cents the unit.

"And so the early evening went. Pick out a fish from the can, tear out the spinal cord — if you weren't Norwegian, eat the whole works if you were. By 7 p.m., the roomers all had red and yellow sauce dripping from their chins and their dress shirts were covered with Nabisco crumbs. Grandma and Grandpa's answer to an elegant cocktail party.

"Finally I moved on to bigger and better things — and

smaller sardines. The 'brisling' variety, with 30 to a small can, and packed in delicate oil.

"Eight years ago, when I began eating lunch with friends at the Little Wagon, I thought I had died and gone to Fisheater's Heaven. For several years I ate the 'Sardine Special' almost every noon. A can of brisling sardines dumped on a plate, with bread and butter and sliced onions. And a plastic tomato, which the chef could have forgotten about.

"Then tragedy struck. The wholesale price of sardines went up 10 cents a can, and management struck the offering from the menu. Sardine fans at our table complained, offered to pay anything management asked to make up for the price increase. No soap. Er, no sardines.

"Yesterday, Little Wagon sardine lovers staged a reunion. I gathered with two other fellows, Gerry Wollan and Tom Lee, who in their years of dining at the establishment, must have eaten up half the population of the North Atlantic. We brought our own sardines. We gave them to Annabelle the Waitress to decant as we chatted about our fragile lives that have perched precariously on the edge of countless sardine tins. Annabelle returned with bread and butter and Bermuda onions and a big pile of the little devils. In 10 minutes, oil was running off our chins and our heavy hearts were happy once again, for the first time in years.

"Things have come to a pretty pass when you have to bring your own food into a restaurant. But in this case it was worth it."

So what, you may ask, does this have to do with the Power of the Press?

Here's what. Three days after the column above appeared in Grit, I ambled over to the Little Wagon, wishing I'd have had the foresight to bring along a can of King Oscar sardines for my lunch.

I sat at the table, waiting for the gang, when up came Little Wagon co-owner, Jerry Benda. He's a fine fellow despite his ignorance of the sardine and his close attention to the bottom line. I always treat Mr. Benda with great respect, as he's a former University of Minnesota football player and looks like he's ready to take a Mack truck by its bulldog and throw it it onto the berm. In his paw, er, hand, Benda carried a copy of Grit, perhaps the first copy of that journal that ever made it inside the Little Wagon, where eating takes precedence to reading.

"Wood, you rat," said Benda. "We slave in the kitchen, we agonize over this joint's decor, we lecture our waitresses to be extremely courteous, all to to make life pleasant for you journalists because we know you have difficult jobs and delicate palates." He pondered the south wall, which was paneled in ply-wood back in 1947. "And what," Benda continued, "do you rats in return?" Then he flung down onto the formica table the column that made his restaurant infamous to all sardine loving Grit readers.

"Do you subscribe?" I asked, politely.

"Subscribe, hell!" said Benda. "One of my friends does and he sent it to me, with some humorous remarks about the quality of our restaurant."

The moment of truth.

What was I to do?

A)Cut and run, with a breadstick hanging out of my gaping maw?

B)Roll up my sleeves, spit on my palms and prepare to read Benda the rules of the Marquis of Queensberry?

C)Snivel and cower and beg his forgiveness?

D)Tell him how very special the chicken salad was at yesterday's lunch?

At this juncture in my life, the press, as I represented it, didn't seem powerful at all.

But, gentle reader, it's always darkest before the dawn, to coin a phrase. As I was calculating how long it would take to make it to the 4th St. exit — with my breadstick intact, of course — Benda leaned down over my table.

(Jeeze, he didn't want to arm wrestle, did he?)

Benda leaned down and whispered the sweetest words I've ever heard:

"On Monday, there'll be a case of sardines out in the kitchen. We're not putting them on the menu, mind you. Just ask Annabelle, whenever you want a can."

"Oh, Benda," I replied, "May the ghost of Good King Oskar look kindly on your menus, on your decor, on your waitresses, even on your chicken salad. May the Little Wagon become a model for the most successful franchise since Mr. Kroc opened his second McDonald's. May you and your partner Dan Mramer be assured of a spot at center grill, when you go up to that Big Stainless Steel Kitchen in the Sky!"

What was I talking about?

After all these years, I still hadn't realized the power of the press or at the very least had forgotten about it. I'd forgotten how Walter Winchell used to stride into the Stork Club, while owner Sherman Billingsley bowed and scraped, knowing his club could be made or broken by the journalist with jaunty felt hat. Benda should have brought me a complimentary cocktail, for gosh sakes.

I had forgotten about how the New York Times drama critics can send a wonderful stage play to oblivion after the first night or how Time magazine can upset half the North American continent by naming a Soviet premier its Man of the Year. Or how the a jaundiced look from the Wall Street Journal can send a company reeling toward bankruptcy.

And so I pulled myself together, squared my shoulders, proud of my role in the sardine caper and proud to be a member of the Fourth Estate. I looked Jerry Benda straight in the eye and with an edge of arrogance in my voice, and asked him the question of the moment.

"How's the chicken salad today? Is it fresh?"

"It's left over from yesterday."

I thought of the Great Masters of Communication, who shine down so brilliantly on the pages of our history:

Horace Greeley, Richard Harding Davis, H.L. Mencken, Walter Lippman.

I thought of Benjamin Franklin walking through the streets of Philadelphia, on his way to becoming a great writer-editor.

I thought of Citizen Tom Paine's "Common Sense."

I thought of my rights under the First Amendment.

I thought of their English language predecessors, Addison and Steele, whose Spectator and Tatler, set London on its ear.

I thought of pamphleteers like Daniel Defoe and Jonathan Swift.

I thought of John Milton's triumphant argument for freedom of the press in his magnificent essay, "Areopagitica." Ah, who can forget that blind bard's immortal words?

*He that can apprehend and consider vice with all her baits and seeming pleasures, and yet abstain, and yet dfistinguish, and yet prefer that which is truly better, he is the true wayfaring Christian.*

Pretty good, huh? But don't forget the best part:

*I cannot praise a fugitive and cloistered virtue, unexercised and unbreathed, that never sallies out and sees her adversary, but slinks out of the race where that immortal garland is to be run for, not without dust and heat.*

Yes, I thought of Milton, who should, as Wordsworth said, be with us now. And I also thought of of lunch.

And so I said to Jerry Benda, football player, concerned restauranteur, unwilling sardine purveyor and my waiter for the moment, "I'll have that, with a slice of Bermuda onion on the side. And maybe a dill pickle?"

# toasty notes

# toasty notes

*toasty notes*

# About the Author
## Whose Mother Was an Arsonist

DAVE WOOD is book review section editor and "On Books" columnist for the Star Tribune in Minneapolis. He also writes "Dave Wood's Column" for Grit, the national family weekly published in Pennsylvania. He was born in 1936 in Whitehall, Wis., and holds a Ph.D. in 18th-century British literature from Bowling Green University in Ohio, where he won both a presidential scholarship and a Danforth Fellowship.

Before embarking on a full-time career in journalism, Wood taught English literature and writing from 1959 to 1980 at Augustana College, Wisconsin State University, Illinois State University, Ball State University, Bowling Green State University and Augsburg College, where he was voted distinguished faculty member of the year in 1972.

In 1973, the Wisconsin Newspaper Association awarded Wood first prize for best local column in the state. His articles on life in the Upper Midwest have since appeared in the Washington Post, The Western Viking, *Nordiske Tidende*, Mpls. St. Paul magazine, Twin Cities Magazine, Wisconsin Trails Magazine.

Many of Wood's articles have been reprinted in various Midwestern regional anthologies, and translations of his work frequently appear in various publications in Scandinavia.

His first book, "Wisconsin Life Trip," appeared in 1976, as did "Telling Tales Out of School." In 1978, he published "Wisconsin Prairie Diary," a history of Western Wisconsin based on his great-grandfather's diaries. In 1985, he and Star Tribune colleague Peg Meier wrote "The Pie Lady of Winthrop".

A board member of the National Book Critics Circle, Wood lives in south Minneapolis with his BW (beautiful wife), Ruth Pirsig Wood.